SORRENTO
VISITING PARADISE
a literary guidebook

Edited by
Anna Tuck-Scala, Ann L. Plamondon, Linnea Vacca

Franco Di Mauro Editore

ISBN 88-87365-13-X
© Copyright 2000 by Franco Di Mauro Editore s.r.l.
Via Fuoro, 30 - Sorrento - Napoli
Printed in Italy
Proprietà letteraria riservata
1ª edizione luglio 2000

Acknowledgments and Copyrights

ISAAC BABEL. Excerpts from *Isaac Babel: The Lonely Years*. Permission granted by Farrar, Straus and Giroux to reproduce the following excerpts: "Naples, April 13, 1933", "Sorrento, April 15, 1933" and excerpts from "Sorrento, April 18, 1933", "Sorrento, April 24 1933", "Sorrento, May 2, 1933", "Sorrento, May 5, 1933", and "Sorrento, May 11, 1933" from ISAAC BABEL: THE LONELY YEARS 1925-1959 edited by Nathalie Babel. Translation copyright © 1962, renewed 1992 by Farrar, Straus & Giroux, Inc. Reprinted by permission of Farrar, Straus and Giroux, LLC.

NORMAN DOUGLAS. The excerpt "Mr Marion Crawford" from *Looking Back*. Permission granted by The Society of Authors as the literary representative of the Estate of Norman Douglas.

NORMAN DOUGLAS. Excerpts from *Siren Land*. Permission granted by The Society of Authors as the literary representative of the Estate of Norman Douglas.

MAKSIM GORKY. Excerpts from *Selected Letters*. © Selection, translation and editorial material Andrew Barratt and Barry P. Scher 1997. Reprinted from Maksim Gorky: *Selected Letters* selected, translated and edited by Andrew Barratt and Barry P. Scher (1997) by permission of Oxford University Press.

HENRIK IBSEN. Excerpts from *The Correspondence of Henrik Ibsen*. Reprinted by permission of Haskell House Publishers.

FRIEDRICH NIETZSCHE. Letter from *Elisabeth Nietzsche, Friedrich Nietzsche: Briefe, Januar 1875-Dezember 1879*. Reprinted by kind permission of Walter de Gruyter & Co.

MARY SHELLEY. Excerpts from *The Letters of Mary Wollstonecraft Shelley*, pp. 77-79, © 1988, The Johns Hopkins University Press. Reprinted by permission.

HERBERT M. VAUGHAN. Excerpts from *The Naples Riviera*, pp. 221-248, © 1925, Methuen Publishing Limited. Reprinted by permission.

COSIMA WAGNER. Excerpts from COSIMA WAGNER'S DIARIES, Vol. I: 1869-1877, translated by Geoffrey Skelton, copyright © 1977 by R. Piper & Co. Verlag Munchen, English translation copyright © 1980 by Geoffrey Skelton and Harcourt, Inc., reprinted by permission of Harcourt, Inc.

A Note of Thanks

This volume is affectionately dedicated
to our friend and mentor,

Portia Prebys

whose kindness and generosity are
as deservedly legendary as her gioia di vivere.

The authors are grateful to all those who helped this volume take shape. To Saint Mary's College at home and in Rome, for providing the stimulus and occasions for persons as diverse and far-flung as the authors to become true colleagues. To Portia Prebys, the Director of Saint Mary's Rome Program, for all her help and support also reflected, however inadequately, in the dedication to this volume. To the Saint Mary's College Library in South Bend, Indiana, for supplying research space without which a collaborative project like ours could not have been undertaken. To the Library's Director Sister Bernice Hollenhorst and endlessly resourceful librarians Robert Hohl and Jill Hobgood, for their perseverance however daunting the task. To the cadre of librarians at the University of Notre Dame Rare Book Room, for skillful reproducing of precious old materials. To Joyce Perry in South Bend and James Zarr in Rome, for their ongoing good humor and exceptional competence in the face of international faxing, fragile texts, and perplexing complications. To the Villa Vergiliana in Cuma, for providing a haven with exactly the right kind of English-language library. To Professor Vicente Berdayes, for sharing his formidable mastery of document scanning. To Ellen Burchenal, Maryland Institute College of Art Sorrento Program, for sharing her expertise and enthusiasm. To Gianfranco Capodilupo, for offering a wealth of stunning photographs for us to choose from. And, finally, to our husbands: Felice Scala, plant pathologist at the University of Naples, Paul Rathburn, Shakespeare scholar at the University of Notre Dame, and Robert Vacca, classicist at the University of Notre Dame. Their support has been unflagging, as too their willingness to interrupt their own professional lives to help us with dogsbody work for this project. Thank you all.

Table of Contents

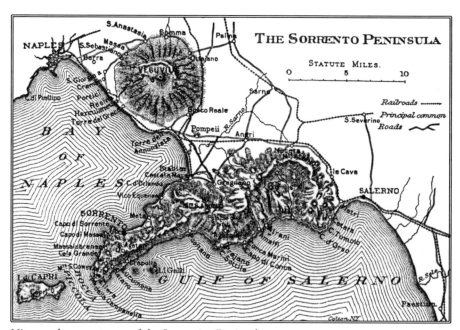

Nineteenth-century map of the Sorrentine Peninsula

INTRODUCTION

It is the stranger, the foreigner, who cannot be silent about Italy; who admires and raves, and, whilst he talks, the Italian hears him with a calm, provoking smile, that says plainly, you may praise her if you like it; I need not. She is mine, and for ever.

JULIA KAVANAGH

Sorrento's natural beauty is siren-like, and visitors have found it irresistible. Rocky mountains jut into the blue Mediterranean sea, lush gardens and fragrant citrus groves overwhelm the senses. Sorrento's renowned hospitality and exceptionally mild climate, as well as its convenient location close to Naples, Pompeii, Capri, and the Amalfi coast, draw tens of thousands every year.

Plaques on hotels and on public walls boast of the notable people who have been drawn to this sea town. Our curiosity was piqued as we noticed how very many of these foreign visitors were writers. What were their reasons for coming here? What did they do while they were here? How did Sorrento seem to *them*?

Today's sophisticated travelers try to go beyond the picture postcard or the practical guidebook to learn something more substantial about the places they visit. Our intention in writing *Sorrento: Visiting Paradise* is to enrich the modern visitor's experience by providing the first English-language literary companion to Sorrento.

We began our search with the local notices and publications listing foreign travelers to the area. Benito Iezzi's *Viaggiatori Stranieri a Sorrento* and *Sorrento e la Sua Storia* were indispensable starting points. As we gathered more information, we were surprised to discover that several well-known writers who wrote about visiting Italy, such as J. W. Goethe, Stendahl, and Charles Dickens, left few written impressions of Sorrento. On the other hand, lesser-known writers, like Julia Kavanagh and Herbert M. Vaughan, for example, offer penetrating insights based on extensive contact with the local culture.

The foreign writers in this volume come from several countries, including France, Germany, Great Britain, Norway, the former Soviet Union, and the United States. Most are Anglo-Saxon and belong to the nineteenth century, when the Grand Tour experience became more accessible and Sorrento enjoyed its Golden Age of tourism. We found that the reflections of writers from this period were particularly valuable because they visited in a quieter time, when life in Sorrento had none of the qualities of a modern tourist town. We hope that the reader will find in the writings of these earlier visitors an opportunity to catch a glimpse of a Sorrento which may not be visible at first glance and to experience, at least imaginatively, a sense of other possibilities.

The passages incorporated into this volume were chosen from a wide variety of writings: novels, essays, guidebooks, letters, diaries, poems. Most were excerpted from larger works, but some works are included in their entirety. We opted to preserve the passages' flavor by presenting them as they were written in their time period rather than standardizing spelling, grammar, or punctuation. Taken together, the selections contribute to an overarching theme which struck us as being implicit in much of the material: the myth and reality of Sorrento as the earthly paradise.

Sorrento: Visiting Paradise begins with an overture – a sampling of praises of Sorrento as "earthly paradise." Chapter Two contains accounts of getting to Sorrento when "getting to" was half the fun, or maybe twice the misery – arduous and possibly dangerous. The aspects of Sorrento most noteworthy to foreign visitors are treated in Chapter Three: its fame as the birthplace of Torquato Tasso, the evocative ruins of Villa Pollio Felice, the historic, picturesque Marina Grande, and the half-obliterated but still fascinating Gorge that cuts through the town. These "monuments" draw out contemplative or moralizing tendencies in some of our authors. In contrast, the selections in Chapter Four simply revel in a sensual enjoyment of Sorrento, the warmth, the scents, the breezes, the tastes, the sheer physical "feel" of the place.

Interestingly enough, the actual inhabitants of Sorrento often face short shrift in travel writings about the place. Chapter Five provides descriptions of the local people and their customs. Often humorous, or perhaps embarrassing, cultural collisions occur in some passages, sometimes also with colonialist overtones. Chapters Six, Seven, and Eight offer a look at the world of some of the visitors – the world and the customs they bring with them, forming cultural microclimates in Sorrento's paradise. The Anglo-Saxons Marion Crawford and Norman Douglas, the Norwegian iconoclast Henrik Ibsen, the Russian revolutionaries Maksim Gorky and Isaac Babel, and the Germanic Richard and Cosima Wagner and Friedrich Nietzsche grapple with lofty issues and personal conflicts while Sorrento serves as the backdrop. Chapter Nine reveals the "other side of paradise," the clash between visitors' expectations and its actuality. The book concludes with an essay by an American, Portia Prebys, who has lived in Italy for decades and who here records her impressions of Sorrento today.

Panoramic view of Sorrento

CHAPTER 1

"THE EARTHLY PARADISE"

*The earthly paradise, I suppose, must look about like the Capo di
Sorrento. The emerald sea is spread out before the window, olive,
orange and lemon groves grow right up to the door. It's only now
that I'm recovering my senses after so much blissful beauty...*

ISAAC BABEL

Praises of Sorrento come in as many varieties as its visitors do. But a
clear overall theme emerges: This is paradise!

HARRIET BEECHER STOWE, *Agnes of Sorrento* (1890)

The town of Sorrento itself overhangs the sea, skirting along rocky
shores, which, hollowed here and there into picturesque grottoes, and
fledged with a wild plumage of brilliant flowers and trailing vines, descend
in steep precipices to the water. Along the shelly beach, at the bottom, one
can wander to look out on the loveliest prospect in the world. Vesuvius
rises with its two peaks softly clouded in blue and purple mists, which
blend with its ascending vapors, – Naples and the adjoining villages at its
base gleaming in the distance like a fringe of pearls on a regal mantle.
Nearer by, the picturesque rocky shores of the island of Capri seem to pul-
sate through the dreamy, shifting mists that veil its sides; and the sea shim-
mers and glitters like the neck of a peacock with an iridescent mingling of
colors: the whole air is a glorifying medium, rich in prismatic hues of enchantment.

...

... In fact, the climate of Southern Italy and its gorgeous scenery are
more favorable to voluptuous ecstasy than to the severe and grave warfare
of the true Christian soldier. The sunny plains of Capua demoralized the
soldiers of Hannibal, and it was not without a reason that ancient poets
made those lovely regions the abode of Sirens whose song maddened by its
sweetness, and of a Circe who made men drunk with her sensual fascina-
tions, till they became sunk to the form of brutes. Here, if anywhere, is the

lotos-eater's paradise, – the purple skies, the enchanted shores, the soothing gales, the dreamy mists, which all conspire to melt the energy of the
will, and to make existence either a half doze of dreamy apathy or an awak-
ing of mad delirium.

F. Marion Crawford, *To Leeward* (1892)

They had been married two months when they came to stay in Sorrento.
It is a beautiful place. Perhaps in all the orange-scented south there is none
more perfect, more sweet with gardens and soft sea-breath, more rich in
ancient olive-groves, or more tenderly nestled in the breast of a bountiful
nature. A little place it is, backed and flanked by the volcanic hills, but having before it the glory of the fairest water in the world. Straight down from
the orange gardens the cliffs fall to the sea, and every villa and village has a
descent, winding through caves and by stairways to its own small sandy
cove, where the boats lie in the sun through the summer's noontide heat, to
shoot out at morning and evening into the coolness of the breezy bay.
Among the warm, green fruit trees the song-birds have their nests, and
about the eaves of the scattered houses the swallows wheel and race in
quick, smooth circles. Far along through the groves echoes the ancient song
of the southern peasant, older than the trees, older than the soil, older than
poor old Pompeii lying off there in the eternal ashes of her gorgeous sins.
And ever the sapphire sea kisses the feet of the cliffs as though wooing the
rocks to come down, and plunge in, and taste how good a thing it is to be
cool and wet all over.

Arthur H. Norway, *Naples, Past and Present* (1901)

... Sorrento, the very name whispers of smiles and laughter, and the people, softening it still with the incomparable music of their speech, modulate
it into "Surriento," just as they turn "cento" into "ciento," and drop a liquid vowel into the harshness of Castellammare, calling it "Castiellammare."
"Surriento!" How it trembles on the air! Had ever any town a name so fit
for love!

And was any ever set in a fairer country? It is a plain, yet no monotony
of level, for a spine of the encircling hills tilts the gardens to the evening
sun, while the shadow of the mountains wards off the fierce glare of the
heat till long past noon. And what fertility! Is there on the surface of the
earth such a lush wild glade of orange groves, three generations, "father,

Lemon trees

son, and grandson," as the Sorrentines say, hanging on a single tree; while as they hang and ripen, the scented flowers are continually budding in the shadow of the dark green leaves, and every waft of air is sweetened by the fragrance of the blossom. But at Surriento all the airs are sweet. If they do not blow across the orange groves they carry down the scent of rosemary and myrtle from the mountains, which are knee-deep in delicious scrub; or they come off the sea in sharp, cool breezes, bringing the gladness and fresh movement of the deep, scattering the stagnant heats and making all the plain laugh with pleasure in the joy of life. How long the lovely summer lasts at Surriento, and how short are the bad winter days!

JOHN RUSKIN, *Diaries* (1841)

February 26th [1841]. Sorrento

A lovely drive yesterday from Castellamare to Sorrento... all lovely rock promontory, orange and olive, and Vico placed *ad captandum* – thoroughly delicious... I set off for a sketch, through the lines of dead wall which border the road to the village... *Dead* walls, by the by, they are not, for their vegetation is so rich and living as to make them rather banks than walls. It was a bright, fluctuating, watery sunlight; the air blue and clear with fresh rain... The oranges wet with the rain, hanging luxuriant in gold and blossom and perfume, over the weedy walls; the village most lovely, one of the most wonderful bits of Italian landscape I have yet seen.

MARY WOLLSTONECRAFT SHELLEY, *The Letters* (1843)

[Sorrento, 20 June 1843]

... I grieve so soon to turn Northward. This place is quite a Paradise – & suits me excellently. The climate of Florence disagreed with me... but here all is smiling. The place is beautiful beyond expression – The weather exactly one's *beau ideal* – warm & no heat – We live comfortably & well & with economy & I have no trouble. I go about on mules in the evenings – [my son] Percy walks by my side – & the exercise does him good – sometimes we go on the sea – We should make a few more excursions if we had more money – & then Percy would be content & I should be quite happy – But alas! we leave this place – too soon – & I plunge again into the shadows & worries of life!... to England I must go – dark, friendless, ungrateful England! Where I have not a tie – not a friend – not an attraction...

[Sorrento, 30 June 1843]

... the reason of our leaving this Paradise is that Percy *will* return to England... Otherwise we should have staid here – where I am happier & better & far more economically than I could be elsewhere.

W. J. A. STAMER, *Dolce Napoli* (1878)

The moon being nearly at the full, I repaired... to the flat roof of the villa, whence the view is more extensive than from the belvidere in the garden. Oh the loveliness of these Italian nights! Where is the mortal so apathetic as to be insensible to their charm? On such a night as this I can hardly bring myself to believe that the violet star-spangled vault above me is the same firmament that looks down on my native land; that the great yellow moon is the same moon that shines so cold and silvery on the English landscape; that earth, sea, air, is not that of some other planet millions of miles away from our own right little, tight little island. In England, however fine the night – and that we have many fine ones during our short summer far be it from me to deny – there is almost invariably something wanting to make it perfection: it is slightly damp, or slightly chilly, or it would be pleasanter were there a *leetle* more air. A night such as this – one of a hundred equally fine that we shall have between this and the setting in of the rains in October – I have never yet seen in England: it is perfect, or as near perfection as anything I can imagine. The nights may be warmer in Venus and brighter in Saturn, but these of Sorrento are warm enough and bright enough for me.

HENRY SWINBURNE, *Travels in the Two Sicilies* (1790)

... Of all the places in the kingdom, this is blest with the most delightful climate. It was renowned for it in ancient times: Silius Italicus extols its soft and wholesome zephyrs. At present, it enjoys shady groves, excellent water, fruit, fish, milk, butter, the finest veal in the world, good wine, and almost every necessary of life at an easy rate. Mountains screen it from the hot autumnal blasts. The temper of the inhabitants is said to resemble the climate in mildness. A few inscriptions and reservoirs of water are all the remnants of antiquity it can shew. It derives its name from the residence or worship of the Syrens... Here Torquatus Tasso drew his first breath in 1544: a bard undoubtedly intitled to rank in the foremost line of modern poets...

HERBERT M. VAUGHAN, *The Naples Riviera* (1925)

As summer advances, the delight of bathing in the limpid waters of the Bay is added to the other attractions of Sorrento, whilst many pleasant and profitable hours can be passed in reading or writing during the long mid-day rest in the cool airy carpetless and curtainless rooms, where on the frescoed ceilings there plays the green shimmer of light that penetrates through the closed bars of the *persiani*, the outside heavy wooden shutters that let in the sweet air, but somehow seem to exclude the intense heat. With the approach of sunset and the throwing open of casements to catch the westerly breeze, there comes a delightful ramble, perhaps an excursion on mule-back to the famous convent of the Deserto or some other point of interest; or else a row upon the glassy waters at our feet, to explore "Queen Joanna's Bath," or some strange caverns beyond the headland of Sorrento, well known to our boat-men. That is the true life of *dolce far niente*, but such an ideal existence can only be indulged in during summer time or in late spring...

Sites and Insights for the Visitor

Sorrento is perched on high cliffs which serve as a natural terrace overlooking the sea. The astounding beauty of Sorrento's natural setting may be viewed not only from the numerous hotels but also from the public belvederes or vistas. Enjoy stunning panoramas, cool breezes and gardens with park benches at three different viewing points: the Villa Comunale (with stairs leading to the beach), Piazza della Vittoria, and near the Museo Correale. The historic "Circolo dei Forestieri" (Foreigners' Club) near Piazza Sant'Antonino also has a delightful view. Here foreign visitors are greeted with a particularly warm welcome at the official tourist information office. Perhaps the loveliest panorama of Sorrento itself and Marina Grande is not from a public belvedere but at the outskirts of town along the road that leads to Massa Lubrense. To reach this spot, walk from the town center of Piazza Tasso to the end of Corso Italia. Then proceed upward along the Via del Capo to the area near Hotel Bristol (approximately a twenty-minute walk).

CHAPTER 2

GETTING TO SORRENTO

Travelers to Sorrento nowadays enter the region using the same land and sea routes as did earlier visitors, but access then was certainly more difficult and possibly also more thrilling and picturesque. Compare Swinburne's cruise to today's rapid crossing on the ferry or hydrofoil, Hare's train journey to catching the *Circumvesuviana* railway from downtown Naples to Castellammare, Fitzgerald's carriage drive to a swift trip by bus or car from Naples. And compare Adams' eventful odyssey to a modern scenic drive along the Amalfi coast.

Henry Swinburne came to Italy after a trip through Spain, about which he published an account. His subsequent journey through Italy led to the publication *Travels in the Two Sicilies in the Years 1777, 1778, 1779, and 1780.* Beginning in Bayonne, he sailed from Marseilles to Naples for an extended visit after which he hired a six-oared barge and embarked from Torre dell'Annunziata, coasting by Revigliano, Castellammare, Vico, and landing at Sorrento. His account reveals his lively interest in the geology of the area.

Augustus Hare traveled by rail from Portici to Castellammare, where the tracks ended and one had to rent carriages to Sorrento, as he did. Sybil Fitzgerald traces her excursion by carriage from Castellammare through Vico Equense, Meta, Trinità, Sant'Agnello, to Sorrento. As is so for many travelers, both native and foreign, the path was the same but the experience different. Hare wrote European guidebooks which could be described as offering a substitute for the Grand Tour to those who had to stay home, as well as being a practical guide for those able to travel if perhaps on a budget. He reviews the quality and cost of hotels, the likely price for carriages (it depended on the number of horses or mules) and for boats (it depended on the number of rowers). Sybil Fitzgerald, whose husband Augustine Fitzgerald was painting in the Naples area, describes their trip with a painter's eye, using a palette of colors: green gorges, sapphire sea, silver olive, white dust, blue and yellow butterflies, golden mustard, violet slopes.

J. Howe Adams' graphic account of approaching Sorrento from the south in the 1890s outlines difficulties no longer faced by travelers today. The roadway was not yet continuous, requiring a passage by boat from Amalfi to Prajano before traveling over land from Prajano to Sorrento. The road was isolated, Positano appeared to the worried travelers a kind of "ghost town," and there was genuine fear of brigands. Adams' "wildest of wild roads," the Amalfi drive, may still be dizzyingly spectacular and offer its own thrills for the bus traveler, but it has undergone a transformation since his time.

From Naples by Sea

HENRY SWINBURNE, *Travels in the Two Sicilies* (1790)

Having received an invitation to be present at the opening of some lately-discovered rooms at Stabia, I went thither with a party. On our way we visited Herculaneum and Pompeii. We then traversed the rich plain that lies between Vesuvius and the Sorrentine branch of the Appennines, and came by a gentle ascent to the excavations. Stabia was a long string of country houses, rather than a town; for it had been destroyed by Sylla, and before the reign of Titus, all its rebuilt edifices were overturned by an earthquake. In the catastrophe of seventy-nine, the wind blowing furiously from the north, brought the ashes of Vesuvius upon it; all the country was covered with cinders and rapilli, or small pumice-stones, many yards deep. Towns, houses, and trees, were buried, and their situations remained marked in the plain by hillocks like barrows. Stabia, though six miles from the mountain, was overwhelmed and lost, till it was casually discovered about twenty-eight years ago. The earthquake had so damaged the buildings, that none of them can be preserved; and therefore, as soon as every thing curious is taken out, the pits are filled up again. The ashes penetrated into all parts, and consumed every thing that was combustible.

On our arrival, the workmen began to break into the subterraneous rooms, and, as the soil is all a crumbling cinder, very little labour was requisite to clear them. When opened, the apartments presented us with the shattered walls, daubed rather than painted with gaudy colours in compartment, and some birds and animals in the cornices, but in a coarse style, as indeed are all the paintings of Stabia. In a corner, we found the brass

Marina Piccola

hinges and lock of a trunk; near them, part of the contents, viz. ivory flutes in pieces, some coins, brass rings, scales, steel-yards, and a very elegant silver statue of Bacchus, about two inches high, represented with a crown of vine leaves, buskins, and the horn of plenty.

The brow of this hill affords a rich and varied prospect towards Vesuvius and the gulf.

The company returned to Naples; but I remained all night at Torre della Nunziata, a large village belonging to the princes of Valle and Dentici, and a hospital. It was of little note while the high road from Naples passed between Vesuvius and Nola, the communication by land along the shore being impeded by repeated eruptions. All that tract was for many ages one dark forest, successively consumed by fiery torrents, and springing up again upon the old cooled lavas. As soon as a road was opened over Herculaneum, the Torre became populous. A manufacture of fire-arms was established here by the present King of Spain, who attempted to introduce several others into the kingdom; but every branch that required nicety, patience, and fine touches, failed: that of arms succeeded wonderfully; and, in three years, the German artificers, he had sent for to instruct his subjects, returned to their own country: for their pupils were become as skilful as themselves.

Early next morning, I hired a six-oared barge, and rowed along the coast. We passed before the island of Revigliano, a fine object, that has been introduced into many pictures. My first station was Castelamare di Stabia, a long town lying at the bottom of the bay, sheltered to the south by high mountains, that come so near the water edge, as to leave only a very narrow slip for the buildings, many of which are boldly and beautifully placed on the lower points of the hills. The King has a charming villa above the city, formerly a farm of the Jesuits. The port is small and entirely artificial, more frequented by Latin sail-barks than ships. This place rose by the ruin of the inland towns. In 1654, the French, under the Duke of Guise, took it by storm, and meant to push their conquests from hence into the heart of the kingdom. Their hopes were soon blasted by a defeat on the banks of the Sarno, which obliged them to reimbark, and abandon even Castelamare, but not before they had stripped it of every thing valuable. I continued my course westward under a bold shore: new beauties of landscape opened upon me at the doubling of every promontory. The first change of scene was to an uninhabited forest, where white cliffs rise perpendicular out of the deep blue waters: behind them, lofty mountains overgrown with wood. These rocks are calcareous, and furnish Naples with lime. The stones are burnt in the creeks, and the fire supplied with faggots cut in the hills, and flung down on ropes. Along the shore are many strong sulphureous springs.

Vico was my next stage: a little city, in a delightful position, on the brow of a hill, backed by an amphitheatre of mountains. The strata of these eminences incline contrary ways to one centrical point, as if there had originally existed a similar mass in the centre, torn asunder and swallowed up by one of those shocks, which must have often overturned this unstable country. Charles the Second and Joan the First raised Vico out of obscurity, on account of the charms they found in its situation.

On doubling the next projecting rocks, we entered the spacious bay of Sorrento, three miles wide. A semicircular chain of woody mountains incloses a rich and beautiful plain, rather sloping towards the sea, full of white buildings peeping out of the groves. This half-moon terminates in a straight line to the sea, by a bold coast of black perpendicular rocks. It probably formed a portion of a circle, half of which broke off and sunk into the waves. This I believe to have been the case, and that the whole was once the crater of a volcano. All of the soil of the plain is cineritious and its rocks a strong blue lava, except near the east end, where they are of a softer piperino kind. The encircling mountains are composed of regular calcareous layers, that do not join or intermix in the least with the others, but are broken off abruptly all round, as if a place had been scooped out for the reception of the heterogeneous mass, rising suddenly out of the bosom of the earth or waters. Many of these limestone rocks are twisted, as it were, into ropes, exactly in the same manner as some Vesuvian lavas: they have besides so many peculiarities, that correspond with those of the productions of burning mountains, that were it not directly repugnant to the common systems of philosophy, which decide all calcareous substances to be a sediment of the ocean, I should be tempted to believe, that fire had a greater share in the formation of these rocks than is generally allowed. The materials of the lower grounds are beyond doubt volcanical; however, I am confident that, as yet, we are but imperfectly acquainted with the powers of fire, and the metamorphoses it is capable of producing. As we have discovered, that the fumes of sulphur and vitriol can change hard black lava into soft white clay, perhaps we may find out, that some other operation of natural chemistry can convert substances into limestone.

I landed at Sorrento, a city placed on the very brink of the steep rocks that overhang the bay, in a most enchanting situation. It contains fifteen thousand inhabitants, half the population of the whole plain. The streets are narrow; but this is no inconvenience in a warm climate, where carriages are not used, nor any communication with the metropolis practicable by land...

From Naples by Rail and Carriage

AUGUSTUS J.C. HARE, *Cities of Southern Italy and Sicily* (1891)

After leaving Portici, the line of railway intersects the great lava streams of 1794. On the left we still have dilapidated yellow houses, and on the right the blue sea and distant Capri, till we reach –

Torre del Greco (Stat.) (Hotel, *Torre d'Ogrieco*.) A town perpetually destroyed by Vesuvius, and rebuilt on and from its lava streams. Its history has given rise to the Neapolitan witticism – "Napoli fa i peccati, e la Torre li paga" ["Naples sins and Torre pays for it"].

The line now runs nearer the foot of Vesuvius, and the peak of the crater swallows up the view of Monte Somma. The *Convent of Camaldoli* is seen (left) on a volcanic mound beneath the mountain. The domed buildings in the vineyards, the wells with their revolving wheels, and the hedges of prickly pear, give a very eastern character to the country. We pass through a stony wilderness of lava, before reaching –

Torre dell' Annunziata (Stat.) A large fishing-town, with flourishing maccaroni manufactories, where Charles IV. established a great powder manufactory, placing the inhabitants, to their infinite terror, between the dangers of a double volcano of nature and man. There is a beautiful view of the bay from hence, with the islet and ruined fort of *Rovigliano* in the foreground.

A branch line leads, in 10 minutes, from Torre dell'Annunziata to *Castella-mare*, the station for Sorrento. There are crowds of carriages at the station, for which it is necessary to make a bargain. The right prices for Sorrento are – 2 horses, 5 frs.; 1 horse, 3 frs. (*Hotels, Qui-si-sana*, or *Gran Bretagna*, most excellent; in a high situation, with a beautiful view, and walks in the woods behind; pension 12 frs.* *Hotel des Étrangers*, in the same situation. *Reale*, in the town, not far from the railway station.

Castellamare is a large dirty town, situated between the sea and the lower spurs of the Monte S. Angelo. It occupies the site of Stabiae, destroyed by Sulla in the Social War, and overwhelmed at the same time with Pompeii in the eruption of A.D. 79. The castle, which gave a name to the modern town, was built by Frederick II.

Castellamare is a most uninviting place to those who do not ascend by the Hotel Quisisana, through an avenue of ilex, by a very steep hill, to the royal Casino of *Quisisana* (now the property of the Municipio), erected on the site of a palace built by Charles II. of Anjou. Its name was invented by Ferdinand I. The view is glorious of Vesuvius, the plain of Pompeii, and the bay, and there are delightful walks in the many-fountained royal *parco*, or in the *bosco* on the mountain-side, which gives Castellamare an advantage over Sorrento, where all the walks are shut in by walls.

In the summer Castellamare is much frequented for its mineral waters, which are of three kinds – *acqua media*, sulphuric; *acqua rossa*, chalybeate; and *acqua acetosella*, aperient. It is the custom for people with liver complaint to drink half a bottle of the first in the morning; a tumbler of the second, with wine, at midday; and as much as possible of the last in the evening. Delightful excursions may be taken along the mountains on donkeys or on foot, and there are drives along the old Sorrento road, or to the ruined castle of *Lettere* (5 m.), whence there is a lovely view. A longer expedition may be made to the *Cappella di S. Michele*, on the top of Monte S. Angelo. It contains a statue of the archangel, which is said to perspire freely on the first of August, when the blessed dew is collected on cotton-wool by a monk, and distributed in little bottles to the faithful.

---

* The Hotel Quisisana is the best point whence to visit Pompeii – about 2.5 m. distant (carriages 2.5 frs.). In the unhealthy state of Naples, this is a great advantage to those who wish to avoid the hotels in the great city.

The drive of 7-1/2 m. from Castellamare to Sorrento occupies 1-1/2 hr. and is one of the most beautiful in Italy. The road passes beneath the Convent of Puzzano (now a pension – *Puzzano Cottage*) to the *Capo d'Orlando*, which gave a name to the naval victory gained here by Ruggiero d'Oria (July 14, 1299) over the fleet of Frederick II. On the left of the road are precipitous cliffs, overgrown here and there with euphorbia or cytizus.

The carriage rattles over the paved streets of several villages. *Vico (Hotel de Vico)* has a cathedral containing the tomb of Gaetano Filangieri, the famous jurist (1788). After crossing a handsome bridge, in a lovely valley clothed with olives, to the oriental-looking village of *Seiano*, we have a view of Vico, with its bright houses and arches, which has been painted by Stanfield and a thousand other artists. The road now ascends to the *Punta di Scutolo*, and descends through groves of oranges, pomegranates, and olives to *Meta (Pension, Villa di Sorrento)*, at the entrance of the rich *Piano di Sorrento* in which we pass the villages of *Carotto, Pozzo Piano*, and *S. Aniello (Albergo di Cocumella* – pension, 6 frs.), and cross two ravines which will recall the *latomiae* of Syracuse in their walls of perpendicular rock and the rich growth of their carpet of oranges, before reaching *Sorrento*.

> The *Hotels* line the cliff, which abruptly overhangs the sea, and have delightful gardens and orange groves on the land side. They are – *Hotel Vittoria*, outside the entrance of the town, the largest and most pretentious and expensive, but very comfortable; pension, 12 frs. *Hotel d'Angleterre (Villa Nardi)*, quieter and more old-fashioned, approached by a lovely lemon grove; pension, 10 frs. *Hotel Tasso (or Tramontano)*, once the Villa Strongoli, excellent, with a very pretty garden – the older building having been Tasso's house. *Hotel Sirena*, above the port of "Marina Grande" – very good, but anglicised and rather dear. Very reasonable lodgings for the summer may be obtained in many delightful villas in the orange groves near the town.
>
> *Donkeys*, half day, 2 frs.; whole day for the longer excursions, 4 frs. To Scaricatojo, 2 frs.; to Vigna Sersale, 1 fr. 50 c.
>
> *Boats to Capri*: with two rowers, 8 frs.; three to four rowers, 12 frs.; five to eight rowers, 16 frs.
>
> *Carriages*, for the half day, 5 frs.; to Castellamare, 2 horses, 5 frs.; 1 horse, 3 frs.
>
> ...

As we enter Sorrento, we cross a deep ravine on a bridge guarded by a statue of S. Antonino, patron of the city. The town extends along a rocky platform above the sea, which comes up almost close to the cliffs, never leaving more than a very narrow strip of beach...

From Castellammare by Carriage

SYBIL FITZGERALD, *Naples* (1904)

The drives to Sorrento, to Amalfi, to Salerno, may be considered as rivals in beauty, since the comparison of one lovely view of Nature with another seems indispensable to the modern traveller. The drive from Castellamare to Sorrento, winding as it does between terraces of vineyards and orange groves, through the leaves of which the deep blue sea and sky and the violet slopes of Vesuvius are continually visible, is certainly one of the most beautiful in the world. Surely, while driving along this glittering road on an afternoon in late spring, it is impossible to imagine anything softer in atmosphere, or more dreamlike. The vegetation is wildly luxuriant. There are green gorges, vine-clad overhanging rocks, sunny walls with enormous clumps of daisies above, and morning glories and purple wistaria trailing over them all. The mingled gold of the orange-trees where the fruit of the past autumn still gleams among the blossoms of spring follows the white and dusty road. Far beneath, washing over the shining rocks, the sea lies like a sapphire, on which "a thousand rainbows have been thrown and broken"; at moments a breeze sweeps over its surface and darkens it to wine-colour – the very sea of the *Odyssey*.

Every foot of ground that can be reclaimed on the precipitous slopes is terraced and cultivated. Everywhere around us is the shimmering silver of the olive, and often a lovely tracery of shadow is thrown upon the road. Shadows are among the most subtle charms of the South. In the North they are almost uniformly dark; here they are but a transparent lacework, luminous and variegated. Under the olives lies a purple tint as soft as the wings of the dove; and the trembling vine-leaf, eternally fanning itself, throws a shadow as cool as it is pale. Paler still is the shade of the fig-tree, so light that the tree can be planted with impunity among the vineyards, as the ancients knew. As we pass between the houses and walls by the way, a clear blue shade lies across the road like a darkened heaven. Lovely and full of poetry are these shadows of the South.

It was in the 'forties that this road was built by Ferdinand the Second, and until now[1] no modern contrivances have broken into its exquisite remoteness. No railway has whistled near; no tramcar, electric or other, has rushed round its undulating curves. Only the slow-moving oxen, the patient mule, the small and rapid mountain horse, and those absurd teams which combine all three beasts, have beaten up the pumice dust in clouds

[1] The electric tramway is to begin working this year. [Fitzgerald's note.]

along the road. Near Castellamare, in the gay summer season, the road is lined with light carriages and red-plumed horses waiting under the shade of the chestnut trees for the crowds of bathers on the shore. In spring and autumn tourist parties, with their luggage strapped on to their vehicles, pass continually to and fro between Naples and Salerno. The rate at which the horses fly past is unequalled for swiftness in any other country I know of. They whirl along, up hill and down, over the dust-white road between cliff and sea with a rapidity which would have horrified Dr. Johnson quite as much as the rolling gait of a stage coach delighted him. There is, too, a delightful sense of having found a faint element of old-time poetry of travel even along a path which, for the last sixty years, has been beaten by tourists of every kind. Honeymoon couples, for half a century, have loved it. Taine felt that where all was so beautiful "la vie peut redevenir simple comme au temps d'Homère."

Beautiful it must ever be; but the road itself will lose one of its greatest charms with the opening tram-line. Its exquisite stillness will be broken into, and those who have known this strip of coast and delighted in it will miss the quality which is hardest to find along the most noisy of beautiful shores.

Above us, winding over the mountains, is the old mule path which was for centuries the only land link between Castellamare and Sorrento – a path so beautiful that every loiterer round this coast should follow it in the spring, pushing his way at times through overgrown bushes and brambles alive with yellow and blue butter-flies; at times breaking into little stony rock paths, up or down the ravines, or by streams black with tadpoles, tiny "sirens of the ditch," as Tasso calls them. Many a legend of brigandage once haunted this path, about which such delicious calm now reigns.

Within the ten miles of coast-line between the two towns, some seven or eight old Roman towns and fishing villages overlap one another, or hide almost unnoticed within the curves of the shore. The most important is the Roman town of Vico Equesne. In its ex-cathedral are some of the best paintings of Bonito, an eighteenth-century artist and native of Castellamare, whose now-neglected works are scattered all over Naples. Morelli, I believe, made an effort to rescue some of his works from oblivion. There are also some sulphur springs, fitted for modern use, and for nearly a mile the air is full of their faint fumes, pleasanter than the powerful odour of the tanneries outside Castellamare. Some of these springs lie so near the shore that they must surely have been under water before the sea retreated in 79. Now we skirt an unbroken succession of enchanting bays, and a long range of hills sloping down to the sea, the highest S. Angelo, which, thickly clad with chestnut trees, is midway towards Sorrento. Many deep curves do we follow inland; yet we come out almost at the point we entered, distances being curiously deceptive along the whole coast. Passing over the bridge which traverses a wide ravine near Meta, the road runs inland along the side of hills where upwards of thirty terraces may be counted rising from far below in the green depths of the gorge to far overhead. At certain parts of the road little children run to meet us, waving flowers or orange boughs. Like wood-nymphs they run lightly through the white dust with their bare feet, laughing and clamouring for sous. Wearily as this eternal cry falls on the ear, at least it is a delight to see such sun-flushed and smiling faces. In Meta is the house of Gianbattista della Porta, the inventor of the Camera Obscura, and the founder of that fantastically named Academy in Naples, the *Oziosi*. The house was traced a short time past by Signor di Giacomo.

From Meta to the parish of the Trinita, where there is one of the best examples of Ippolito Borghese's work – the Resurrection – we pass through orange groves; then comes the little town of S. Agnello, the land of Giacomo de Castro, many of whose works fill the neighbouring churches. As the danger limits of Vesuvius are distanced, S. Gennarius is forgotten and the more peaceful images of Madonna and Child are around us. We are on a road of Madonna's shrines and legends. They hide under the drooping trellis of leaves at the corners of sunny walls, or rise high against the houses under the creepers. Over one white-washed shrine the ripe oranges tremble under the trees. Over another, marking the turn into a mountain path, roses and wistaria have twined together a web of flowers; and there is yet another, near which the mustard plant glows like gold, while within it there is a tiny natural garden. To the stranger, already filled with the tender charm of this land, these continual and simple signs of religious feeling seem quite idealistic; but many are the romantic illusions in Italy which vanish as we delve beneath its lovely surface. The religion of the poor is but a debased Paganism without the spontaneous spirit of Pagan days. These shrines show the worship of not one Madonna, but of countless local deities, who often change in popularity as easily as the most trifling fashion, and an unanswered prayer will rouse a sentiment of revenge which is often expressed by either totally neglecting the Madonna's shrine or locking it up so that no offerings can reach her. It is the same unreasoning rage with which the Neapolitans insult the bronze statue of their patron saint by terming him "Yellow Face" when the liquefying of the blood is too slow. Unfortunately, the great Madonna-worship about Naples, so full of the natural poetry of the people, is often a means among the dishonest of acquiring money and confiscating the humble offerings of the poor, as in the case of the Madonna della Pignasecca. When one of these frauds was discovered, and all the gifts of the faithful were found to have been squandered in the hands of the Camorristi, a Frenchman asked a poor woman what was the use of money given for such a purpose. "Excellenza," she answered, "we give to the Madonna, and the intention in our heart is a good one; if others steal the money, what does it matter to us?"

A gentle slope leads down to the sheltered table-land on which stands Sorrento, the little town without a history...

From Salerno by Carriage and Boat

J. Howe Adams, *"The Highroad from Salerno to Sorrento"* (1894)

Our route lay from Salerno on the Gulf of Salerno to Amalfi, twelve miles away, thence three miles by boat to Prajano, and thence on to Sorrento by twenty-five miles of the wildest of wild roads. The country below Salerno was flat and uninteresting; southward stretched the dreary waste on which twenty miles away one could fancy that he saw the famous ruined Grecian temples of Paestum, while beyond was *terra incognita* of the truest type, an insignificant marsh that presented no allurements to the most enthusiastic traveler. But to the north and west rose the mountains of St. Angelo, running out into the Sorrentine peninsula, and dividing the Bay of Naples from the Gulf of Salerno. These picturesque mountains, dotted with romantic villas and charmingly situated little hamlets, look down on the soft and dazzling blue waters of the Mediterranean, making that peculiar mystic union where perfect land meets perfect water.

Beginning at Salerno, and skirting this scene from fairy-land, is the famous highroad cut into the surface of the rock for miles, crossing deep ravines by artistic spans of heavy stone that show no suggestion of modern cantaliver, but seem as much a part of the scenery around them as though made by the hand of God. In this land of fine roads it is superlatively fine; broad, sweeping, and as clean and hard as a marble floor. Built in 1852, modern improvements and devices can show no road to excel it; like the scenery, it is perfection.

As we rolled out of Salerno, we could see the road running from promontory to promontory as far as the eye could reach. Occasionally it disappeared up some rocky gorge; but if the eye was keen, a faint, ribbon-like effect could be seen in the solid rock, which betrayed its course. Now the road climbed the mountainside to Capo Tumolo, where the whole scene unfolded like a map at our feet; again it dived down to the water's edge to skirt Capo d'Orso, or crept along the edge of some precipice, from which the village of Cetara could be seen below, stretched along the bottom of a narrow ravine. Now the road penetrated the picturesque towns of Minori, Majori, or Atrani, where it ran between the high white walls of the peasants' houses, under the shadow of which lingered a decided chill and gloom, while for hundreds of feet above the road were the whitest of white houses, hanging to their terraces like overgrown white goats. Everywhere that the eye could see were these terraces; no rock was too barren, no ledge too narrow, no gorge too deep to escape being covered to the very edge with terraces of orange- and lemon-trees. These groves are watched most tenderly, each orange and lemon being frequently tied up in a little paper bag to protect the fruit from insects and the sudden winds, which, notwithstanding the sunniness of the climate, occasionally blow up from the sea.

This region is one of beauty, but not of fertility; a paradise for the rich, but a purgatory to the poor man. The natives must eke out their scanty crops with their fishing-boats. Looking down over the edge of the road in any gorge wide enough to hold some sand and a fishing-smack, one can see the dark houses, and the gaily painted sails and sides of the boats. Human beings live down there, away from sunshine and contact with their fellows, and yet they are light-hearted, sunny children, easily pleased, easily angered, and easily satisfied. It will not do to look below the surface in one of these picturesque villages; disease and ignorance need not be sought far. The houses are dark, damp, and unclean; the inhabitants are miserably poor; the children are rachitic and white-faced. Taxes are certainly the curse of Italy, especially of this southern country. The Italian peasant is taxed fully fifty per cent. of his labor and products; his beds are taxed, his furniture, his windows, his very movements to town and back cost him money – money, to be sure, that builds beautiful roads and holds Italy together as a nation, but still a grievous tax.

Picturesque scenery is hard to farm; fishing with medieval apparatus is slow and poor, especially with no near market to consume the catch. Nature has followed her usual course: to the visitor who has she gives more; but from the native who has not she is taking away his little. But we did not think of this as we whirled along; it is easy enough to moralize when our ride is done, but while we breathed this glorious air, and saw these inspiring sights, we could not conceive that misery could exist in such a country. These people are an uncomplaining race; they are not particularly obtrusive with their woes, although they see possible soldi for miles, and are willing to run as many more to get them.

Our plan, which was the best of many, included a stop at Amalfi overnight; staying there as long as we desired, and then pushing on to Sorrento. Our driver kept up his gait through town after town, through ravine after ravine, past wayside shrine and bubbling fountain, until at last we rolled in triumphant state into that painter's paradise, the world-renowned Amalfi. The first and last impression of this ride to Amalfi was that of sunshine – of sunshine so warm, so unremitting, and so absorbing of energy, that cold and snow seemed utter impossibilities: in this stimulus life had no sorrow or death; beauty and pleasure controlled the senses in this medley of sea and mountain, villa and ravine. This impression was the chief charm of the trip and its brightest legacy, for it increased as the petty annoyances of the avaricious Italian were forgotten; for even here we were reminded of the contemptible human element, although any business and profit-getting seemed strangely out of touch with the place.

There are two Hotels dei Cappuccini at Amalfi, one being the *dépendance* of the other, belonging to the same family. This is another exhibition of the wiliness of the Italian landlord, who is far too bright for the American traveler. The first hotel of this name is down in the town of Amalfi, on a narrow, dark street, shut in from any view except seaward; it is the first one reached by the traveler, however, and unless he has been there before, or is very wary and determined, he will be persuaded by both driver and porter that this is the far-famed Hotel dei Cappuccini of his dreams. But the real Hotel dei Cappuccini is half a mile beyond, as the driver will suddenly remember if one flatly refuses to stop at this little one-horse village inn. He will be amply repaid for making this stand, for here, perched three hundred feet above the road, unapproachable except by a series of white stone steps, stands this unique hotel. In America there would be a huge Kaaterskill perched on such a spot, but the Italians, far more in sympathy with the artistic demands of the surroundings, have turned the one-time famous old Capuchin monastery into a well-appointed home, for home it is for the traveling world. The guests sleep in the cells of the old monks, and dine in the old whitewashed chapel. There is the customary orange- and lemon-grove on a narrow terrace alongside the hotel, flanked by a broad, sweeping path, which afforded the only cloister for the monks, while on the other side of this walk stands a row of white, plastered pillars supporting a roof of arching vines; from here a superb view of Amalfi and the blue Gulf of Salerno lies before the eye. The stairs to the dining-room come down into the room from the sleeping-rooms without intervention of hall or wall, and as we descended these massive whitewashed stone steps, we could see the dining-table stretched along, covered with bright lamps and dainty flowers, while the high-arched roof betrays the old chapel. It was as attractive to the hungry traveler as the mountains on the outside had been to the other senses.

We left Amalfi at three o'clock on a bright, sunny afternoon, in late April. The theatrical little town was sound asleep; its bird-box houses were deserted; its streets were vacant and quiet. The cathedral steps were covered with the morning's work of the washerwomen, doing no nobler duty than that of a place to dry clothes. Such is the use of the beauty and romance of Amalfi to the native. With these garments still on the steps, we took a hasty photograph of the old cathedral of St. Andrew the Apostle, whose remains are said to repose in the crypt beneath it. This cathedral is an interesting example of the style introduced into Italy by the Normans after their conquest of Sicily. The presence of the body of St. Andrew made this spot a place of pilgrimage in the middle ages. "The manna of St. Andrew," oily droppings from his casket, enjoyed a high reputation in southern Europe for its miraculous power in curing disease. Its efficacy has been sung even by the great Tasso.

Our rowboat, which was to carry us from Amalfi to Prajano, three miles away along the coast of the Gulf, lay close to the shore, but no wharf or board to reach its side was in sight. Our wonder was short-lived, however, for suddenly the ladies of the party gave sudden screams, as each was clasped by waist and feet by two sturdy, barefooted boatmen, and before they could protest, they were safe in the little craft.

As we looked back, the little town slept on; the old monastery hotel reflected a dazzlingly sunny glare from its walls and its three hundred feet of steps, while the only living thing in sight was an invalid English woman standing on a balcony of the hotel. As the boatmen rowed, they sang the romantic songs of Italy, with the clearness and beauty which develop only under the Southern sky. They knew grand opera, and such stirring ballads as "Santa Lucia," and "Bella Napoli"; but "Margarita," the song which was sweeping over Italy at the time, named for the popular queen, was unknown to them, showing their separation from the current news of their little world. As we skirted the rocky cliffs, against which the Mediterranean lazily splashed, we saw occasionally a watch-tower gazing out to sea, a suggestion of the days of Barbary pirates and their sudden swooping charges on the hapless peasant of the middle ages. Under the shadow of the rocks grows the bright red, "vegetable coral," the "apples of the sea," a curious form of growth, which attracts the traveler's eye so constantly that the boatmen have learned its English names and habits.

In the year before our journey the road was extended from Positano to Prajano; in a year or so it will be cut through from Prajano to Amalfi, and then the traveler will miss this beautiful trip by boat, which makes a unique part of the journey from Salerno to Sorrento. It will be another instance where improvement in travel will destroy some of its picturesqueness. As we approached the opening ravine in which lies the sheltered fishing-hamlet of Prajano, we saw, dashing down to meet us from all directions, over the rocks and crags, swarms of barefooted women and girls. The men had all gone to Naples or America, looking for steadier work than landing chance passengers. Down came this barefoot, dirty, motley crew, as sure-footed as goats, and running as rapidly. They overwhelmed the passengers, seized the luggage, and made themselves nuisances. No words, gestures, or blows from the boatmen could drive them away. They were as patiently persistent as a swarm of mosquitos; the moment one stopped his expostulation, back they came.

Now we found ourselves in a dilemma, for our carriages, which were to come from Sorrento, had not arrived. In vain did we search the place; the town of Prajano boasted neither an inn nor a horse; we must patiently wait. Five o'clock came, and then six; dusk began to settle on the hills, and we were just deciding to go back to Amalfi, when over a distant point we saw two small carriages traveling along. We were anxious to reach Sorrento, and were assured by the drivers that the ride would be quickly made. Our horses, driven at breakneck speed for twenty-five miles, were in no condition to start back; but start back we did, and soon the town of Prajano was a memory. In ten minutes we reached Positano, where the landings were formerly made before the road was built to Prajano. In the weird, dusky light that appears early under the edge of these precipices, Positano was a ghostly place. No peasants walked the streets; the windows of the houses were knocked out; it looked like a haunted town, or a place dead with the plague. Its oppressiveness was terrible, and we were glad to leave it, and to get out into the healthier desolation of the next ravine.

The road was far wilder than from Salerno to Amalfi. The rocks were higher, the ravines deeper, and after leaving the outskirts of Positano there were no villages. Soon the moon came up, and, while we could not see it, for we were a thousand feet below the upper edge of the cliff, it threw a ghastly light over the sea, which was thrown back into our faces, and made them seem blanched and careworn. We remembered with sudden distinctness that Baedeker speaks of one road in this region which by some good authorities is scarcely regarded as free from brigands; we believed that this was the one. It was a happy, inspiring thought, and we tried to reassure ourselves of it by looking into the guidebook; but the wind blew too hard to keep a match going, and we would not stop our driver for worlds. Soon we went, dipping into ravine after ravine, until the road seemed endless. As we rounded each point, we looked for the place from which we must bend to cross the mountains to Sorrento. Time crawled from seven to half-past seven, to eight. We saw out in the dim distance in the bay the uncertain forms of the Islands of the Sirens, as they are called; we knew that a long stretch still lay before us.

At half-past eight we had settled down to our fate, whatever it was to be, when suddenly we saw the gleam of a light around a neighboring cliff. We had not passed man, bird, or beast since leaving Positano two hours before. This was interesting; who would have a light on this lonely, forsaken road with honorable purpose? But before we could conclude as to the motives of our rapidly approaching friends, we ran into a band of soldiers, tax-collectors, who were looking for peasants smuggling their wares to Sorrento untaxed. They glanced carelessly into our carriage, and allowed us to pass, giving us the first opportunity of our lives of being heartily glad to welcome a custom-house officer. This sudden visitation in this desolation was a pleasant break; it brought life and law back to us again. Nine o'clock came on; but the scenery was gradually changing – the hills grew lower, the vegetation higher. We were evidently approaching the break in the mountains through which we were to reach Sorrento. Soon we left the sea, and pierced the thick underbrush, and started on a dreary climb over the hills. This was worse than the sea, for there no one could approach us from the sea in ambuscade, or from the mountain-side either, for that matter, unless they were more than goat-like in agility. But here were darkness and silence doubly intense. Every tree hid a figure, and the moonlight brought out slinking movements in every bush. Up, up we crawled, until, finally, at nearly ten o'clock, we stood on the summit of the ridge, and the Bay of Naples, glorious in the moonlight, lay at our feet five miles away. In the distance the lights of Naples gleamed, each light with a welcome in it, while closer, under our feet almost, lay the twinkling lamps of Sorrento.

Now came merry work; down the steep hills we bowled, through high-walled roads, past silent villas, until the famous road from Castellammare to Sorrento was reached. Now we laughed our fears to scorn, and when we drove into the yard of the famous Hotel Tramontano at Sorrento, our heads were held up boldly, as though wild drives like this were of daily occurrence.

CHAPTER 3

SORRENTINE ATTRACTIONS

Sorrento's reputation for being a natural paradise has been the primary enticement for visitors to come to this part of Italy. Unlike many other highly sought destinations, Sorrento does not offer an overwhelming array of ancient ruins, museums, and works of art. One foreign writer commented that "Sorrento [is] the little town without a history. Travellers pass through it, but know little or nothing of its past. For them it is the smiling town where oranges, lemons, and olives have ever flourished" (Sybil Fitzgerald, 1904). Another perceptive woman visitor commented "The antiquities of Sorrento... read better than they look... The real antiquities that speak, and have a language both graceful and expressive, are those that are blended with the lives of the people" (Julia Kavanagh, 1858). The most frequented artistic sites of today's visitor such as the Museo Correale di Terranova (opened to the public in 1924), the Sedile Dominova (one of the historic seats of the local nobility), the cloister of San Francesco, and the Duomo and bell tower, are scarcely mentioned in writings by foreign visitors. It is almost as if part of the visitor's experience of paradise comes from the relief of not being weighed down by the daunting burden of Italy's long and productive artistic past.

But there were some attractions that captured the attention of many foreign visitors. The fact that Sorrento sired *Torquato Tasso*, one of the greatest poets of Italy, undoubtedly appealed to visitors who were writers or interested in literature. There is very little left to see of Tasso's life in Sorrento – but this was enough to spur the imagination. The same may be said for *Villa Pollio Felice.* A few ruins are all that remain of this luxurious ancient Roman villa. Yet with the help of a poem by the Latin poet Statius, the visitor can try to resurrect the splendor of Sorrento's ancient past. *Marina Grande* and *the Gorge* have inspired writers to reflect on how a particular landscape can shape and determine one's way of living and viewing life. These "attractions" in the following chapter are not what would commonly be called "monuments to visit" in Italy. They are rather sites that stir the imagination and provoke the visitor to reflect on the passage of time in this natural paradise.

Sorrento, "Cradle of Torquato Tasso"

Torquato Tasso (1544-95), one of the greatest poets of Italy, is Sorrento's most illustrious son; *Gerusalemme Liberata*, his adventure-filled epic on the Crusades, is his most famous work. Tasso spent only a brief period of his life in Sorrento. Still, the obscure little city of his birth became a pilgrimage site for literary visitors. It is said that a few rooms of Tasso's original home are now incorporated into the Hotel Imperial Tramontano. Perhaps this is one of the reasons why writers such as Harriet Beecher Stowe, James Fenimore Cooper, and Henrik Ibsen decided to lodge there during their Sorrentine sojourns. The conjunction of the poet's birthplace and its lofty location on the edge of the cliffs towering over the sea was undoubtedly inspiring to them. Today's visitors may find fascinating the pair of letters below by James Fenimore Cooper; he provides a rare description of the physical characteristics of the exclusive "cradle of Torquato Tasso" and what it was like to stay there in the first half of the nineteenth century.

Two other cities drew writers and visitors who were interested in Torquato Tasso: Ferrara, where Tasso spent time at the d'Este court and was tragically imprisoned in the hospital of Sant'Anna for insanity, and Rome, where his tomb is in the monastery of Sant'Onofrio. The Romantic poets especially were passionate about Tasso's heroic poetry, but they were even more stirred by the unfortunate episodes of Tasso's tormented life. The nature of Tasso's madness and his fear of persecution inspired poetry by Goethe, Shelley and Byron.

Herbert M. Vaughan, who wrote at length about visiting Sorrento in *The Naples Riviera* (1925), presents a lively and thorough overview of Tasso's life and the events that captured the Romantic imagination. One episode in particular may continue to arouse the interest of the visitor to Sorrento. In 1577 Tasso escaped from a period of confinement in a convent in Ferrara and returned after a long absence to Sorrento disguised as a shepherd. He visited his sister, Cornelia, and tested her sisterly affection by greeting her with the news that her brother, Torquato, was dead. She is reported to have fainted with grief; when she revived she was overjoyed when Torquato revealed his true identity. The few days he spent reunited with his sister in Sorrento, the town of their childhood, offered a momentary respite from his misfortunes.

J. W. GOETHE, *Torquato Tasso* (1885)

Goethe's *Torquato Tasso*, set entirely in Ferrara, offers a passage in which Tasso anticipates returning to his birthplace of Sorrento:

> TASSO. I know the danger, and have ponder'd it.
>   Disguis'd I go, in tatter'd garb, perchance
>   Of Shepherd, or of pilgrim, meanly clad.
>   Unseen I wander through the city, where
>   The movements of the many shroud the one.
>   Thee to the shore I hasten, find a bark,
>   With people of Sorrento, peasant folk,
>   Returning home from market, for I too
>   Must hasten to Sorrento. There resides
>   My sister, ever to my parents' heart,
>   Together with myself, a mournful joy.
>   I speak not in the bark, I step ashore
>   Also in silence, slowly I ascend
>   The upward path, and at the gate inquire:
>   Where may she dwell, Cornelia Sersale?
>   With friendly mien, a woman at her wheel
>   Shows me the street, the house; I hasten on;
>   The children run beside me, and survey
>   The gloomy stranger, with the shaggy locks.
>   Thus I approach the threshold. Open stands
>   The cottage door; I step into the house...

WALTER SAVAGE LANDOR, *Imaginary Conversations* (1843)

Landor, a nineteenth-century writer, imagined this dramatic meeting between Torquato and Cornelia. Although the conversation is "imaginary," the descriptions of Sorrento throughout the poem sound as though they were written from first-hand observation.

> CORNELIA. Be calm, be composed, my brother!
> TASSO. You would not require me to be composed or calm if you compre-
> hended a thousandth part of my sufferings.
> CORNELIA. Peace! peace! we know them all.
> TASSO. Who has dared to name them? Imprisonment, derision, madness.
> ...
> ... I woke early in the morning; thou wert grown up and gone. Away to
> Sorrento: I knew the road: a few strides brought me back: here I am.
> To-morrow, my Cornelia, we will walk together, as we used to do, into
> the cool and quiet caves on the shore; and we will catch the little
> breezes as they come in and go out again on the backs of the jocund
> waves.
> CORNELIA. We will indeed to-morrow; but before we set out we must take
> a few hours' rest, that we may enjoy our ramble the better.
> TASSO. Our Sorrentines, I see, are grown rich and avaricious. They have
> uprooted the old pomegranate hedges, and have built high walls to pro-
> hibit the wayfarer from their vineyards...

HERBERT M. VAUGHAN, *The Naples Riviera* (1925)

But the name which above all others Sorrento will cherish as her own, "so long as men shall read and eyes can see," is that of the famous Italian poet, Torquato Tasso, whose interesting but melancholy life-story is closely associated with this, the town of his birth. Tasso is reckoned as the fourth greatest bard of Italy, ranking after Dante and Petrarch, and being esteemed on a level with rather than below his rival and contemporary, Ludovico Ariosto. In one sense however he may be described as the most truly national poet of this immortal quartet, for his career is connected with his native country as a whole, rather than with any one of the little cities or states then comprising that "geographical expression" which is now the Kingdom of Italy. His father's family was of Lombard origin, having been long settled in the neighbourhood of Bergamo, where a crumbling hill-set fortress known as the Montagno del Tasso still recalls the name of the poet's ancestors. His mother, Porzia de' Rossi, was Tuscan by birth, her family haling from Pistoja at the foot of the Apennines, but owning property near Naples; whilst the poet himself was destined to spend his years of childhood at Sorrento and at Naples, his youth at Rome and Verona, his

Torquato Tasso's house (now Hotel Tramontano)

brilliant period of fame and prosperity at Ferrara and the Lombard courts, and again some of his closing years of disgrace and disappointment amidst the familiar scenes of his infancy. Of good ancient stock the Tassi owed their acquisition of wealth to the reestablishment of the system of posting throughout Northern Italy in the thirteenth century, when the immediate progenitor of the poet, one Omodeo de' Tassi, was nominated comptroller, and it is curious to note that owing to this circumstance the arms of the family containing the posthorn and the badger's skin – "Tasso" is the Italian for badger – continued to be borne for many centuries upon the harness of all Lombard coach-horses. Torquato's father, Bernardo Tasso, himself a poet of no mean calibre and the composer of a scholarly but somewhat prolix work, the *Amadigi*, formed for many years a prominent member of that brilliant band of literary courtiers within the castle of Vittoria Colonna, the Lady of Ischia, of whom we shall speak more fully in another place. But for the overwhelming and all-eclipsing fame of his distinguished son, Bernardo might have been able to claim a high place in the list of Italian writers of the Renaissance; as it was, the father's undoubted talents were quickly forgotten in the blaze of his own beloved "Tassino's" popularity, so that he is now chiefly remembered as the sire of a poetic genius, as one of the great Vittoria's favourite satellites and as the author of an oft-quoted sonnet to his intellectual mistress. Bernardo Tasso did not marry until the somewhat mature age of forty-seven, when, as we have already said, he espoused the daughter of the Tuscan house of Rossi, by whom he had two children; a daughter, Cornelia, and the immortal Torquato, who was born in 1544, three years before the death of the divine poetess of Ischia.

But Bernardo was not merely a bard and a courtier, for he was also, unfortunately for himself and his ill-fated family, a keen politician in an age when politics offered anything but a safe pursuit, and as his views invariably coincided with those of his chief friend and patron, the head of the powerful Sanseverino family, Tasso the Elder found himself in course of time an exile from Neapolitan territory on account of his dislike of the new Spanish masters of Naples. The poet-politician therefore took up his abode at Rome, whilst his wife and two young children continued to reside at Naples and Sorrento. The boy was a born student, almost an infant prodigy of learning, and so great was his desire for knowledge that he would insist upon rising long before it was day-light, and would even make his way to school through the dark dirty streets of Naples, conducted by a servant with a torch in his hand. The Jesuits, who had just set up their first academy at Naples, soon discovered in the future poet an ideal pupil, and not only did they impart to the child all the lore of ancient Greece and Rome, but they also imbued his mind, at an age when it was "wax to receive and marble to retain," with their own peculiar theological tenets. It is obvious indeed that the faith implanted by the Fathers in his tender years was largely, if not wholly answerable for the unswerving belief and firm religious convictions that ever stood Tasso in good stead throughout the whole of his chequered career. "Give me a child of seven years old," had once declared the great founder of the Society of Jesus, "and I care not who has the after-handling of him"; and in this case the Jesuit professors did not fail to carry out Loyola's precept. But his home life with his mother, whom he loved devotedly, and his course of study at the Jesuit school were suddenly interrupted when he was barely ten years of age, for the elder Tasso was anxious for his little son to join him in Rome, there to be educated under his own eye. The boy left his mother, but after his departure the Rossi family brutally refused to allow their sister access to her absent husband, who had lately been declared a rebel against the Spanish government and deprived of his estates. Thus persecuted by her unfeeling brothers, Porzia Tasso sought refuge together with Cornelia in a Neapolitan convent, where, deprived of her erratic but beloved husband and pining for her absent son, the poor woman died of a broken heart a year or two later. As for Cornelia, she became affianced when of a marriageable age to a gentleman of Sorrento, the Cavaliere Marzio Sersale, and consequently returned to live in the home of her childhood.

Of Tasso's many adventures, of his universal literary fame, of the honours heaped upon him by his chief patron, Duke Alfonso of Ferrara, and of his subsequent disgrace and imprisonment for daring to lift his eyes in love to a princess of the haughty House of Este, we have no space to speak here. Let it suffice to say that he was one of the most charming, virtuous, brilliant, manly figures, as he was also almost the last true representative, of the great Italian Renaissance, the end of which may be described as coinciding with his decease. According to his biographer Manso, the author of the *Gerusalemme Liberata* was singularly noble and refined in appearance, though always possessed of an air of melancholy; he was well-built, strong, active and resourceful, anything in fact but a carpet-knight who spent his days in writing verse and dallying with Italian court beauties:

"Colla penna e colla spada,
Nessun val quanto Torquato;"

sang the populace of Ferrara in honour of their illustrious Sorrentine guest, for the Ferrarese delighted in the handsome stranger who could in an emergency wield the sword as skilfully as he could ply his quill. Twice only however did Tasso revisit the city of his birth, and each return home was occasioned by deep tragedy. In 1577, wounded by the attacks of his literary rivals and humiliated by the Duke Alfonso's discovery of his infatuation for the Princess Leonora d'Este, the unhappy poet travelled southward, reaching Sorrento in the disguise of a shepherd. Making his way to the Casa Sersale, the house of his sister, now a widow with two sons, Torquato passed himself off as his own messenger, and so eloquently did he relate the story of his own grief and wrongs, that the tender-hearted Cornelia fainted away at this recital. Having satisfied his mind as to his sister's genuine affection, the pseudo-shepherd now revealed his true character, whereupon the pair embraced with transports of joy, though it was deemed prudent not to acquaint their friends with the arrival of Torquato, who was represented to the good people of Sorrento as a distant relative from Bergamo. Cornelia Sersale now entreated the poet to take up his abode permanently in her house, and to forget the rebuffs of the cruel world without in the enjoyment of family ties and affections; and well would it have been for Torquato, had he accepted his sister's advice and passed the succeeding years in simple rural pleasures. But restless and inconsequent despite all his virtues, the poet must needs return to Ferrara to bask in the presence of his beloved Leonora, with the dire and undignified result that all the world knows. Tasso's second visit took place not long before his death, when his

Balcony of Cornelia Tasso's house

strength was rapidly failing, so that it seems strange that he did not decide to end his days amidst these lovely and well-remembered scenes of his early boyhood, instead of deliberately choosing for the last stage of his earthly journey the Roman convent of Sant' Onofrio, where the death-chamber and various pathetic relics of the poet are still pointed out.

Students of Tasso's immortal epic are apt to overlook the immense influence exercised on its author by his early Sorrentine days and surroundings. The *Gerusalemme Liberata* contains, as we know, a full account of the First Crusade and constitutes an apotheosis of Godfrey de Bouillon, first Christian King of Jerusalem; but it is also something more than a mere poetical description of a departed age of chivalry. For there can be little doubt that the poet aspired to be the singer of a new movement which should wrest back the Holy City from the clutches of the Saracens, and set a second Godfrey upon the vacant throne of Palestine. To this important end the experiences of his infancy and his training by the Jesuits had undoubtedly tended to urge the precocious young poet. The servants of his father's house at Sorrento must many a time have regaled his eager boyish mind with harrowing tales of the infidel pirates who scoured the Tyrrhene Sea within sight of the watch-towers on the coast; within ken, perchance, of Casa Tasso itself, perched on the commanding cliff above the waters.

Scarcely a family dwelling on the Marina below but was mourning one or more of its members that had been seized by the blood-thirsty marauders, perhaps to be brutally slain on the spot or to languish in the dungeons of Tripoli and Smyrna, eking out a life of slavery that was far worse than death itself. Stories of tortured Christians, like that of the pious Geronimo of Algiers who was tied with cords and flung into a mass of soft concrete, were common enough topics among the Sorrentine folk, all of whom lived in constant dread of a successful raid by the Barbary pirates. For, despite the efforts of the great Emperor Charles the Fifth to protect his maritime subjects, the swift galleys of Tunis and Tripoli out-stripped the Imperial men-of-war, and continued to carry on their vile commerce of slavery. Such a state of terrorism must have appeared intolerable to the

Statue of Torquato Tasso in Piazza Tasso

highly romantic, deeply religious spirit of the young poet; and his Jesuit preceptors, working on the boy's imagination, were soon able to instil into his youthful brain the notion of a new Crusade which would not only sweep the infidel ships from off the Italian seas, but would also recapture the Holy City itself. The Church, beginning at last to recover from the effects of Luther's schism, was once more in a position to re-assert its ancient authority over Catholic Christendom, and in Torquato Tasso it found an able trumpeter to call together the scattered forces of the Faithful, and to reunite them in a holy war. Astonished and delighted, all Italy was swept by the golden torrent of Tasso's impassioned verses, that were intended to urge the Catholic princes of Europe to the inauguration of a new Crusade. Nor were the times unpropitious for such an event. Tunis, that hot-bed of infidelity, piracy and iniquity, was in the hands of the Christians; and the fleets of the Soldan had been well-nigh annihilated by Don John of Austria at the glorious battle of Lepanto: – to convince a doubting and hesitating world that the actual moment had come wherein to recover the city of Jerusalem was the main object of the author of the *Gerusalemme Liberata*.

And it was his infancy spent upon this smiling but pirate-harassed coast that was chiefy responsible for this desired end in the epic of the Crusades; it was Tasso's early acquaintance with the Bay of Naples, combined with his special training by the Jesuits, that forced the poet's genius and ambition into this particular channel.

It is pleasant to think that Sorrento is still appreciative of its honour as the birth-place of the great Italian poet. The citizens have erected a statue of marble in one of their open spaces; they have called street, hotel and *trattorria* by his illustrious name; and can the modern spirit of grateful acknowledgment go further than this? His father's house has perished, it is true, through "Nature's changing force untrimmed," for the greedy waves have undermined and swallowed up the tufa cliff which once supported the old Tasso villa. But there is still standing in Strada di San Nicola the old Sersale mansion, wherein the good Cornelia received her long-lost brother in his peasant's guise, an unhappy exile from haughty Ferrara. Of more interest however than the old town house of the Sersale family is the ancient farm, known as the Vigna Sersale, which once belonged to Donna Cornelia, and supplied her household with wine and oil. It is a lovely sequestered spot lying on the breezy hill-side not far down the Massa road, facing towards Capri and the sunset. Hallowed by its historic connection with the poet and his devoted sister, the Vigna Sersale can claim perhaps to be one of the most interesting and beautiful places of literary pilgrimage upon earth. Ascending by the steep pathway that leads upward from the broad high road, it is not long before we reach the old *podere*, amidst whose olive groves and vineyards the poet was wont to sit dreamily gazing at the glorious view before him. Here are the same ancient spreading stone-pines, the same gnarled olive trees that sheltered the gentle love-lorn poet, whilst Cornelia and her sons sate beside him in the shade, endeavouring – alas! only too vainly – by their caresses to detain the roving Torquato in their midst. Could not, we ask ourselves, the erratic poet have been content to remain in this spot, "in questa terra alma e felice" as he himself styles it, instead of plunging once more into the dangers and dissipation of that Vanity Fair of distant Ferrara? Why could he not have brooded over his ill-starred infatuation for the highborn Leonora in this soothing corner of the earth, allowing its quiet and beauty to sink into his soul, until the recollection of his Innamorata declined gradually into a fragrant memory that could be embalmed in never-dying verse? But like his own favourite hero, the Christian King of Jerusalem, the poet must in his inmost heart have preferred a changing storm-tossed life to the ideal existence of rustic ease; and had he not returned to the treacherous splendours of Alfonso's court, how much less entrancing would his own life-story have appeared to after ages! Unconsciously he seems to have composed his own epitaph in describing Godfrey's death; for the crusading king lived and died like a true Christian knight, for whom the world has afforded many adventures, and but few intervals of peace until the final call to endless rest.

JAMES FENIMORE COOPER, *Excursions in Italy* (1838)

From Letter XIII

It is not an easy thing to find a residence for a family that has no material objection... The choice was finally made at Sorrento, a town of a few thousand inhabitants, directly opposite to Naples, and at the distance of eighteen miles. The house we took has a reputation from having been the one in which Tasso was born, or, at least, *is said* to have been born; and although it is not the villa of Cardinal Ruffo, it is little inferior to it in scenery. The greater part of the plain on which Sorrento stands is surrounded in a half circle by mountains, the segment facing the bay. The whole formation is volcanic, large fissures of the tufa appearing in the shape of deep ravines in various places. Advantage was taken of the accidental position of these ravines, so as to form a deep natural ditch around most of the place, which stands on the immediate margin of the plain. This plain is six or seven miles in length, is a continued village, very fertile, and extremely populous. Its elevation above the bay varies from one to two hundred feet, the verge being a perpendicular cliff of tufa nearly the whole distance. Sorrento lies near the south-western extremity, the heights overlooking it. The house we have taken is on the cliffs, within the walls, and in plain sight of every object of interest on the bay, from Ischia to the promontory of Vico, Castel-a-mare and a short reach of the coast in its vicinity excepted.

Letter XIV

We did not get into our residence at Sorrento until the 20th of August, and here we have now been several weeks. Everybody is delighted with the place, and I think we have not in any other abode, in or out of Europe, enjoyed ourselves so much as in this. The house is not particularly elegant, though large; but as it has a name, and may be taken as a specimen of an Italian country abode, I shall describe it.

To begin at the foundation, ours rests on narrow shelves of the cliffs, which cliffs, just at this spot, are about one hundred and fifty feet in perpendicular height, or possibly a little more. It has a treacherous look to see the substratum of a building standing on a projection of this sort; but I presume sufficient heed has been taken to security. Of this substratum I know but little, though there appear to be two or three stories down among the cliffs. All the dwellings along these rocks, many of which are convents, have subterraneous communications with the sea, the outlets being sufficiently visible as we row along beneath the heights. The government, however, has caused them to be closed, without distinction, to prevent smuggling.

The house forms two sides of a square, one running inland, and the other standing on the extreme verge of the cliffs, as you will readily understand when you remember that the foundations rest on the places I have just mentioned. We occupy the principal floor only, although I have taken the entire house. There is a chapel beneath the great *sala*, and I believe there are kitchens and offices somewhere in the lower regions; but I have never visited any portion of the substratum but the chapel. We enter by a gate into a court, which has a well with a handsome marble covering or curb, and a flight of steps fit for a palace. These two objects, coupled with the interest of Tasso's name, have been thought worthy of an engraving. From the *loggia* of the great stairs we enter into an ante-room of good dimensions. Inland is a still larger room, in which we dine, and another within that again, which is the only apartment in the house with a fireplace. By the presence of the chimney, it is fair to presume the kitchen is somewhere at hand. This room W... has for a bedroom. Seaward, two or three vast ante-chambers, or rooms *en suite*, lead to the *sala*, which faces the water, and is a room fifty feet long, with width and height in proportion. The furniture is no great matter, being reduced to the very minimum in quantity; but it is not unsuited to the heat of the climate and a *villeggiatura*. There are old-fashioned gilded couches and chairs, and a modern divan or two to stretch our limbs on. There are also some medallions and busts, antiques: one of the former, on what authority I cannot say, is called an Alexander the Great. The windows of the *sala* open on the court, on the street, and on the sea. A street that leads among convents winds toward the great landing and the bay.

Towards the water there is a little terrace, which forms the great attraction of the house. It is only some fifty feet long, and perhaps half as wide; but it hangs over the blue Mediterranean, and, by its position and height, commands a view of three fourths of the glorious objects of the region. It has a solid stone balustrade to protect it, massive and carved, with banisters as big as my body. This renders it perfectly safe, as you will understand when I tell you that, hearing an outcry from P... the other day, I found him with his head fast between two of the latter, in a way that frightened me as well as the youngster himself. It was like being embedded in a rock.

As I sit at the foot of the dinner table, I look, through a vista of five large rooms, by means of doors, at the panorama presented by Naples, which town lies directly across the bay, at the reputed distance of eighteen miles; though I see St. Elmo so distinctly, that it appears not half as far. Of course, when seated on the terrace, the view is infinitely more extended. The sea limits it to the west. Ischia, dark, broken, and volcanic but softened by vegetation and the tints of this luxurious atmosphere, comes next: then Procida, low, verdant, and peopled. The misty abrupt bluff of Misenum is the first land on the continent, with the Elysian fields, the port of the Roman galleys, and the "Hundred Chambers." The site of delicious Baiae is pointed out by the huge pile of castle that lies on the hill-side, and by the ruined condition of all the neighbouring objects of curiosity, such as the Sibyl's cave, the lake of Avernus, and the bridge or mole of Agrippa. Behind a little island called Nisida, the bark of St. Paul must have sailed when he landed at Puteoli, on his way to Rome. The palace of Queen Joan, the grotto of Pausilippo, the teeming city, and the bay dotted with sails, follow. Then the eye passes over a broad expanse of rich level country, between Vesuvius and the heights of the town. This is the celebrated Felice Campania, with Capua in its bosom; and the misty background is a wall of broken rocks, which in form are not unlike our own palisadoes, but which, a grand range of the Apennines, have probably six or seven times their height. These mountains, at times, are scarcely visible, just marking the outline of the view in a sort of shadowy frame, and then, again, they come forth distinct, noble, and dark, the piles they really are. On particular days they do not appear to be a dozen miles from us. I have seen them already, more than once, glittering with snow, when they are indeed glorious. The base of Vesuvius, a continued hamlet of white edifices, including palaces and cottages, with its cone for the background, follows; and a pile of dingy earth, or ashes, just marks the position of Pompeii.

There is a little room partitioned off from the terrace, that I use as a cabinet, and where I can sit at its window and see most of these objects. The distance impairs the effect but little; for so great is the purity of the atmosphere, at times, that we have even fancied we could hear the din of Naples across the water. In all this, too, I have said nothing of the movement of the bay, which is getting to be of great interest.

Sites and Insights for the Visitor

Torquato Tasso's birthplace has apparently been assimilated into the Hotel Imperial Tramontano. The exterior of this spot described by James

Fenimore Cooper can be seen from Piazza della Vittoria. In 1858, accord-
ing to Julia Kavanagh, this was "the only memorial the people of Sorrento
have preserved of their illustrious citizen." In fact, only with the unifica-
tion of Italy in the 1860s did the town administration finally name a
street after its poet. The Via Tasso corresponds to the cardo maximus *(the*
principal north-south axis of the Greco-Roman town of Surrentum). A
monument to Torquato Tasso by Gennaro Calì was erected in Piazza
Tasso, the main square and heart of town (1866). During this period of
the nineteenth century, increased civic pride and the renewed interest in
Torquato Tasso generated by the Romantics coincided with intensified in-
ternational tourism in Sorrento. Many distinguished guests fled harsher
winter climates to stay in Sorrento's elegant hotels for extended periods.
Most of the foreign writers who show interest in Torquato Tasso and left
impressions about Sorrento belong to the nineteenth century.

It is still possible to visit the site of Tasso's dramatic meeting with his
sister in 1577. Off Via Fuoro, at Via San Nicola, number 11, stands Casa
Fasulo (not open to the public), once the home of Tasso's sister, Cornelia
Sersale. Cornelia married Marzio Sersale in 1558, the year Sorrento was
attacked by Turks. The Turkish action may have been a source of inspira-
tion for Gerusalemme Liberata, *Tasso's epic about the Crusades. At Casa*
Fasulo, note the Sersale coat of arms above the portal and the delightfully
bizarre mannerist balcony on the first floor. The sculpted grotesque faces
peer down at the visitor and playfully stick out their tongues.

Of interest to bibliophiles will be the Museo Correale's collection of
old and rare editions of Tasso's works. A bookstore called "Libreria
Tasso," on Via San Cesareo, sells books and maps that may enhance the
visitor's stay in Sorrento.

Villa Pollio Felice

HENRY SWINBURNE, *Travels in the Two Sicilies* (1790)

... I continued my coasting voyage to Capo di Terra, or Puolo, the point
that divides the bay of Sorrento from that of Massa. Here are the ruins of a
villa mentioned in Statius's Sylvae [see appendix]: it belonged to Pollius
Faelix, whose name is still preserved in the modern appellation. I admired
the exactness with which the poet has described the spot; for however al-

Aerial view of Villa Pollio Felice

tered and disfigured the minuter features may be, the great outlines of the place are still discernible. On the very extremity of the Cape, impending over the sea, stands a row of vaulted chambers, before which appear the vestiges of a portico, or hall. Its form is that of an obtuse angle. These rooms commanded a double view; one of Sorrento and Vesuvius; the other, of Naples, Puzzoli, and Ischia. Part of the painting remains upon the walls. Behind these buildings, the promontory narrows into an isthmus, pierced in the middle with a deep round bason, into which the sea has access by a passage under the rocks. As the waves have no force left when they enter it, and its opening is surrounded by ruins, this was no doubt the situation of the baths. Three arched conduits brought fresh water to them from a large reservoir at the foot of the mountain; high rocks, covered with olive-trees, defend this place from the boisterous scirocco, and boats find a safe retreat in a circular creek, which divides the cape into two peninsulas. From hence I sailed along the woody coast of Massa...

ARTHUR H. NORWAY, *Naples, Past and Present* (1901)

There can, I think, be few districts in which the folklore is richer or more romantic than in this region of Sorrento. The peasants are soaked in superstition. The higher classes are scarce more free from it. Those who loiter at midnight near the Capo di Sorrento, whither every tourist goes to see the ruins of the Villa Pollio and the great cool reservoir of sea-water known as "Il Bagno della Regina Giovanna," may see a maiden clad in white robes rise out of the sea and glide over the water towards the Marina di Puolo, the little beach which lies between the Punta della Calcarella and the Portiglione. She has scarce touched land when she is pursued by a dark rider on a winged horse, who comes from the direction of Sorrento, and hunts her shrieking all along the shore...

JULIA KAVANAGH, *A Summer and Winter in the Two Sicilies* (1858)

... The promontory, which is called Capo di Sorrento, and which stretches into the sea between Sorrento and Massa, still keeps on a rock daily beaten by the sea waves, and round which, on stormy days, they boil and foam furiously, the shattered relics of an ancient temple formerly consecrated to Hercules. Other ruins, said to be those of the villa of Vedius Pollio and of an amphitheatre, mingle with the fragments of the temple... The spot is a favourite one with painters. The ruins make a picturesque foreground, and Capri, invisible from Sorrento, appears in purple outlines on the horizon of sea and sky.

...

... All the antiquities of Sorrento... read better than they look. The archaeologist alone is privileged to take delight in the names of buildings and temples, in the sites on which they stood, and in a few old stones which may be called ruins... The real antiquities that speak, and have a language both graceful and impressive, are those that are blended with the lives of the people...

...

... Near the Punta del Capo, exist the ruins of what was once the haunt of a siren more beautiful and more dangerous than any of whom Homer sang. I am not learned enough to say which Queen Joanna she was, but I have taken it for granted that she was the beautiful one. Here, therefore, Queen Joanna had her baths. This lonely spot – those cool green waters – beheld the sweet and wonderful beauty which Leonardo da Vinci painted...

...

... We passed underneath the irregular arch, and entered a circular space where the sea flows, with walls of rock and a roof of blue sky.

The sun still shone on the green heights of the hill above, but cool shadows slept on the water below. Carmela bent curiously over the edge of the boat, and far down in the clear deep bed she saw crumbled masonry, and dark rocks, and green sea-weeds, and young crabs, and fine sand, and did not seem to me to care or to know whether Queen Joanna had ever bathed here or not. I spoke to her of the past, and gave her a historical account of the death of King Andrew; but one of the little crabs swimming briskly around the boat shared her attention with my words. Perhaps Carmela thought, "I am twenty-three, and living; and I am worth all the dead queens and dead beauties." Perhaps she thought nothing, and merely enjoyed the brown rocks, the emerald waters, the serene sky, ever beautiful, and doubly beautiful with nature and solitude. But, though silent, she was none the less impressed. This passeggiata, one of the few pleasures she has ever enjoyed, will remain a memorable event in her quiet life.

...

... For this is the mischief of Italy, that all sorts of classical thoughts and heathen dreams and stories which leave one quiet enough in cold northern countries, here run into one's head at every turning...

Sights and Insights for the Visitor

Ancient Sorrento was known as "Surrentum," a name that invokes the song of the sirens. People have lived here from very early times, but only a few traces of Roman ruins remain for the visitor to see today without the aid of an archaeologist. Recent excavations in front of Villa Fiorentino on Corso Italia have revealed ancient Roman structures; more remains certainly lie hidden beneath much of today's historic center as well. The decumanus maximus *or east-west main axis of Surrentum, which led to the Roman forum, corresponds to today's Via San Cesareo and Via Fuoro ("fuoro" derives from "foro" or* forum*) and the* cardo maximus *or north-south axis is along Via Tasso. Walking around the narrow streets of this part of town, the visitor may discover fragments of ancient columns and capitals incorporated into later walls and buildings. Highly recommended is the Museo Correale di Terranova (the Correale Museum) which houses an archaeological section as well as many other art treasures.*

The Roman villa known as Villa Pollio Felice *is exceptional not only as one of the few visible testimonies of Sorrento's ancient Roman past but also because it proves how the Romans admired and inhabited the most beautiful sites along the coasts of this region. Long before the modern phenomenon of mass tourism, many wealthy Romans came to the Bay of Naples, Capri, and the Sorrentine peninsula and sought out the choicest spots to vacation and build their summer residences. Sorrento's fame as a lovely place for visitors is quite ancient.*

Like Henry Swinburne, today's visitor can explore what is left of the ancient walls and foundations of the Villa Pollio Felice (first century A.D.) with Statius' poem in hand (see appendix). This Latin poet, Publius Papinius Statius, praises both the villa and its wealthy and cultured owner, the Roman senator Felix Pollius, in the full-blown rhetoric expected of poets by patrons. He marvels at the villa's "numberless summits and changing views" and notes that each chamber "has its own delight, its own particular sea... each window commands a different landscape." Reading Statius' celebration of this luxurious private residence, the visitor can imagine living in pampered luxury on the very edge of the glorious sea.

The natural scenery surrounding the Villa Pollio Felice is so very beautiful that the pleasant walk to visit it becomes a real treat. The end of the cape offers sweeping panoramas of sea, Vesuvius, and Sorrento. The area is a popular summer swimming spot. In a natural basin adjacent to the Villa Pollio Felice, the sea penetrates an opening in the rocky walls and forms a small shimmering pool of radiant green. Sorrentines refer to this site as the "Bagni della Regina Giovanna" (Queen Joan's Baths), the name also mentioned in the above passages by Arthur H. Norway and Julia Kavanagh. The French queen of Naples (1343-1382, House of Anjou), Giovanna may have frequented this bathing spot. Both her beauty and her cruelty were legendary and apparently left a lasting impression on the Sorrentines. Indeed this magical place to swim becomes a lonely place in the wintertime, filled with the haunting and fearsome beauty that is traditionally associated with the infamous queen.

Directions: *From the Villa Comunale belvedere in Sorrento, one can see the Capo di Sorrento – the small rocky promontory crowned with the ancient Roman ruins of "Villa Pollio Felice" jutting out into the sea. The best way to reach it is to drive or take the local bus towards Massa Lubrense and get off at Via del Capo (about a six-minute ride). Then walk along the narrow, uneven stone road which descends rather steeply through citrus groves and olive trees and ends at Punta del Capo, the tip of the promontory (approximately a fifteen-minute walk).*

Statius, Silvae, Book II.2
(First Century A.D.),
"The Villa of Pollius Felix at Surrentum"

Between the walls that are known by the Sirens' name and the cliff that is burdened by the shrine of Etruscan Minerva a lofty villa stands and gazes out upon the Dicarchean deep; there the ground is beloved of Bromius, and the grapes ripen on the high hills nor envy the Falernian wine-presses. Hither was I glad to come after the four-yearly festival of my home, – when at last deep quiet had fallen and the dust lay white upon the course, and the athletes had turned them to Ambracian garlands, – drawn by the eloquence of gentle Pollius and bright Polla's girlish charm to cross my native strait: though already fain to direct my steps where runs the worn and well-known track of Appia, queen of the long roads.

Yet the time I spent delighted me. The crescent waters of a tranquil bay break through the curving line of cliff on either hand. The spot is of Nature's giving: one single beach lies between sea and hill, ending towards the land in overhanging rocks. The first charm of the place is a smoking bath-house with two cupolas, and a stream of fresh water from the land meeting the salt brine. Here would the nimble choir of Phorcus wish to bathe, and Cymodoce with dripping tresses and sea-green Galatea. Before the building the dark-blue ruler of the swelling waves keeps watch, and guards that innocent home; his shrine is it that is wet with friendly spray. Alcides protects the happy fields; in the two deities does the haven rejoice: one guards the land, the other resists the angry billows. A wondrous peace is on the sea: here the weary waves rage no more, and the furious South wind blows more mildly; here the swift hurricane is less daring, and the pools lie tranquil and undisturbed, calm as the spirit of their lord.

Thence a colonnade climbs slantwise up the cliff, vast as a city, and its long line of roof gains mastery over the rugged rocks. Where the sun once shone through clouds of dust, and the way was wild and unlovely, now it is a pleasure to go. Even such, should you scale the lofty height of Bacchic Ephyre, is the covered way that leads from Lechaeum, of Ino's fame.

Not if Helicon were to grant me all her streams, or Pimplea quench my thirst, or the hoof of the flying steed abundantly assuage it: not if mystic Phemonoë were to unlock her pure springs or those wherein my Pollius, under the auspices of Phoebus, hath plunged his deep-immersed urn – not even so could I equal in Pierian strains the countless charms and beauties of the place. Scarcely could my eyes sustain the long array, scarce could my feet avail, while I was led from scene to scene. What a multitude of things! Shall I first admire the genius of the place or of its master? This part of the house looks eastward to Phoebus' morning rays; that part detains him as he sets, nor allows the exhausted light to disappear, when the day is wearied out and the shadow of the dark mountain falls on the waters, and the proud mansion floats upon the glassy flood. Here the sound of the sea is in the chambers, here they know not the roaring of the waves, but prefer the silence of the land. Here are spots that Nature has favoured, here she has been outdone and given way to the settler and learnt gentleness in ways unknown before. Here, where you now see level ground, was a hill; the halls you enter were wild country; where now tall groves appear, there was once not even soil: its owner has tamed the place, and as he shaped and conquered the rocks the earth gladly gave way before him. See how the cliff learns to bear the yoke, how the dwellings force their entry and the mountain is bidden withdraw. Now let the skill of Methymne's bard and that sole Theban lyre and the glory of the Getic quill give way before thee: thou too dost move the rocks, thee too the high woods follow.

Why should I tell of ancient forms in wax or bronze, or of aught that the colours of Apelles rejoiced to animate, or the hand of Phidias carved, though Pisa still was empty, yet wondrously withal, or what was bidden live by Myron's art or Polycletus' chisel, the bronzes, from the funeral fire of Corinth, more precious than gold, countenances of chieftains and prophets and sages of old time, whom it is thy care to follow, whose influence thou dost feel in all thy being, untroubled and steadfast in thy tranquil virtue, and ever lord of thy own heart? Why should I recount the numberless summits and the changing views? Each chamber has its own delight, its own particular sea, and across the expanse of Nereus each window commands a different landscape: this one beholds Inarime, from that rugged Prochyta is seen; here the squire of mighty Hector is outspread, there sea-girt Nesis breathes tainted air; yonder is Euploea, good omen for wandering barks, and Megalia flung out to repel the curving billows; and thy own Limon grieves that his lord reclines there over against him, and gazes at thy Surrentine mansion from afar. Yet one room there is, one higher than all the rest, which over a straight track of sea brings Parthenope to thy sight: here are marbles chosen from the heart of Grecian quarries; the stone of Eastern Syene, splashed with veining, and that which Phrygian axes hew in mournful Synnas o'er the fields of wailing Cybele, whereon the white expanse is bordered by a rim of purple; here too are green blocks quarried from the hill of Lycurgus at Amyclae, where the stone counterfeits the grass; here gleam the tawny rocks from Numidia, Thasian marble too and Chian, and Carystian stone that joys to behold the waves: all turn to salute the Chalcidian towers. A blessing on thy heart, that thou approvest what is Greek and hauntest Grecian land; nor let the city of Dicarchus that gave thee birth feel envy! We shall prove better owners of our poet-ward.

Why should I rehearse the wealth of the countryside, the fallows flung out into the sea and the cliffs steeped in Bacchus' nectar? Often in autumn-time when the grapes are ripening a Nereid climbs the rocks, and under cover of the shades of night brushes the sea-water from her eyes with a leafy vine-spray, and snatches sweet clusters from the hills. Often is the vintage sprinkled by the neighbouring foam; Satyrs plunge into the water, and Pan-gods from the mountain are fain to grasp the sea-nymph as she flies naked through the waves.

Bless with prosperity, O land, thy lord and lady both, unto the years of a Nestor or a Tithonus, nor ever change thy noble servitude! Let not the Tirynthian hall and Dicarchus' bay outdo thee as a home, nor thy lords too often gladden the wistful vineyards of Laconian Galaesus. Here where Pollius plies his Pierian craft, whether he ponders the Gargettian teacher's counsels, or strikes my own lyre, or unites unequal strains, or draws the threatening sword of avenging satire: the nimble Siren speeds from these rocks to sweeter lays than hers, and here Tritonia lifts her head and listens. Then the wild winds abate, the seas themselves are forbidden to rage; the dolphins emerge from the deep, and drawn to the music of his harp float gently by the cliffs.

Long mayst thou live, enriched beyond Midas' wealth and Lydian gold, blest above the diadems of Euphrates and of Troy; whom neither fickle power nor the shifting mob, nor laws nor camps can vex, whose great heart, raised sublime over all desire, doth quell hope and fear, who art beyond the will of Fate and dost baffle the enmity of Fortune; thee the last day shall find, not bewildered in the maze of things, but sated with life and ready to depart. But we, a worthless folk, slaves at the beck of transient blessings and wishes ever new, are tossed from chance to chance: thou from thy mind's high citadel dost look down upon our wanderings and laughest at human joys. There was a time when the loyalty of two lands tore thee in twain, and thou wert borne in triumph through two cities, there worshipped, as is meet, by Dicarchus' folk, here made their own by mine, and bountiful alike to these and those, in the full fire of youth and proud of thy wandering Muse. But now are the mists dispersed, and thou dost behold the truth – others in their turn are tossed upon that sea – and thy unshaken bark has entered a peaceful haven and a quiet resting place. Continue thus, nor ever loose thy vessel, her voyage over, to face our storms. And thou, who in wisdom dost surpass the daughters of Latium and in mind art equal to thy lord, whose spirit no cares, whose brow no menace has dismayed, but who art ever bright and happy, while joy untroubled reigns in thy countenance: – for thee no churlish money-chest keeps tight grip of hoarded wealth, no waste of greedy usury tortures thy heart, but open to all are thy riches, and thou dost enjoy them in wise restraint. No union of souls is more blest, such are the minds that Concord has taught. Learn of her in untroubled peace, ye from whose hearts the blending fires are met in a long union, and whose hallowed love keeps fast the laws of chaste affection. Go onward through the years, and outdo the centuries of old and the title-roll of ancient fame.

Marina Grande

HERBERT M. VAUGHAN, *The Naples Riviera* (1925)

Unlike other towns upon the Bay of Naples, Sorrento is divided into two distinct portions; the city on the cliffs, with its streets and squares, its cathedral and ancient walls, its villas and gay gardens; and the Marina, lying at the mouth of the gorge below, close to the water's edge. The population of Upper Sorrento is agricultural and labouring, whilst that of the lower consists entirely of fisher-folk and sailors; it is needless to add that the latter are far less prosperous than their fellow-citizens who live overhead. Until recent times little communication between these two sets of Sorrentines took place and intermarriages were rare, for the sea-faring population only ascended to the town above and intermingled with the people of Upper Sorrento on the great occasions of local festivals, such as the enthronement or funeral of a bishop. Nor has the levelling spirit of the age as yet broken down the deep-rooted feeling of local clannishness; although it cannot be long before time-honoured customs and prejudices will be swept away in the tidal wave of modern development...

ARTHUR H. NORWAY, *Naples, Past and Present* (1901)

... Immediately below me is a little beach, the Marina Grande, the opening of the westerly ravine, small, yet much the largest which the town possesses, and there most of the boats lie hauled up on the black sand. An-

Marina Grande

other fringe of lava sand runs under the dark cliff below the great hotels. Sometimes in the early morning the traveller, waking not long after dawn, may hear a low monotone of chanting down beneath his window, and flinging it open to the clean salt wind that breathes so freshly over the grey sea dimpling into green, ere yet the sun does more than sparkle on the water, he will see far down below him the barefooted women tugging in the nets, while the fish glitter silvery on the red planking of the boat that rocks on the translucent water twenty yards from shore.

HENRY SWINBURNE, *Travels in the Two Sicilies* (1790)

... In 1558, the Turks sacked this city, and carried off twelve thousand captives; but, preferring money to such a quantity of slaves, they sent to Naples to ask a ransom. Distrust, consternation, or insensibility, caused their offer to be rejected, and the infidels sailed away with their prisoners. Soon after, by an act of generosity scarcely to be paralleled in any history, the remaining Sorrentines sold their lands and goods, and redeemed their fellow-citizens. Had such an effort been made by Greeks or Romans, it would have been a common-place example for school-boys, and every dissertator, ancient and modern, would have enlarged with enthusiasm on this trait of heroism; but at Sorrento it is scarcely remembered, and, I believe, it is entirely forgotten in the rest of the kingdom.

Sites and Insights for the Visitor

Sorrento has two marinas: Marina Piccola and Marina Grande. The former, teeming with travelers, is the primary port for ferries and hydrofoils to Naples, Capri, the Amalfi coast, and other destinations. Marina Grande, in sharp contrast, is a self-contained, picturesque fishing community. It can be reached in less than ten minutes by walking along Via Marina Grande from Piazza della Vittoria. Near the end of this enchanting road the visitor may notice the Villa Tritone where Benedetto Croce, a renowned Italian philosopher and historian, stayed during World War II. The road then becomes a stepped cobblestone pathway descending steeply and winding through the charming dwellings and the portal of Marina Grande. This gateway was the only entrance from the sea to the town of Sorrento up until the fifteenth century. In 1558, the Turks ("the barbaric infidels") broke through the natural fortress of the cliffs and sacked the town of Sorrento as described by Swinburne. Even today Marina Grande is associated with the Turkish invasion in the Sorrentine popular imagination.

As Vaughan notes, Marina Grande is quite close to Sorrento but is considered a distinct community with its own identity, culture, and traditions. The visitor may savor the authentic atmosphere of this small cove with its cluster of pastel houses, fresh seafood restaurants, and boats along the shore. The women of Marina Grande often call to each other in dialect across their balconies while hanging out their laundry. Children play in front of the church of Sant'Anna and fishermen bring in their catch or repair their nets and boats. This little community is a paradise for stray cats whose main concerns are napping in the sun and cadging scraps of fish.

The patron saint of Marina Grande is the protectress of sailors, Sant'Anna the mother of Mary. Her feast day is July 26th and it is celebrated with a procession on the Sunday following. The men of Marina Grande in traditional sailor garb transport the venerated statue of Anna holding her daughter Mary's hand. The procession winds from Marina Grande through the streets of Sorrento. Not to be missed either are the boisterous popular festivities associated with this feast day: concerts, local food stands, and on the last day (usually Monday), a sensational fireworks display on the sea.

A note for enthusiasts of Italian cinema: Marina Grande (as well as Marina Piccola) is the setting for the classic Italian movie, "Pane, amore e..." ["Bread, love and..."] (1955) directed by Dino Risi and starring Sophia Loren and Vittorio De Sica.

The Gorge

SYBIL FITZGERALD, *Naples* (1904)

... Part of this piazza [Tasso] is built over the great gorge beginning in the hills and descending rapidly to the sea, and once a roaring torrent must have dashed down the ravine. The line of the old town wall of mediaeval times which once followed it has now disappeared and has given place to a fine road. Crumbling ruins are incongruous in Sorrento, and the hand of man has not been idle in helping to remove them...

ARTHUR H. NORWAY, *Naples, Past and Present* (1901)

So high and dark is this ravine that though the sun is almost exactly above it, its light catches only the bushes at the very top, and penetrates not at all into the sheer funnel down which the water plunges, scattered into spray by the force of the descent, until a hundred feet below it drops upon a jut of rock and so pours down in a succession of quick leaps from pool to pool.

It is a wild and beautiful sight to watch the downpour of this water on the days succeeding rain. But in the warm weather the ravine is dry, and an active climber might go up it without much trouble. There is some temptation to the feat; for men say a treasure lies hidden in a cave which opens out of sheer walls, and the gold is enough to make a whole village rich. If any doubt it, let him go there on the stroke of midnight. As the hour sounds, he will see the guardian of the hoard appear at the top of the ravine, a dark mailed warrior, mounted on a sable steed, who leaps into the gulf and vanishes when mortal men accost him...

...

It is a pleasant spot at this hour of evening shadows. The deep ravine is filled with the whispering echoes of a stream, which does not fill the bottom of the hollow, but leaves space for orange groves, deep thatched with boughs. Cottages are built out on jutting rocks, overhanging the precipice with strange indifference to the probable results of even little earthquakes; and the lanes are alive with brown, half-naked children. The sheer rocky chasms, the swarming population, the ancient walls, recall memories of an older Sorrento than one can recover easily upon the sea-front, or in the tortuous streets which skirt it. One sees here the system of defence, and can believe that in its day Sorrento was a fortress, though its great days of independence passed so early...

HARRIET BEECHER STOWE, *Agnes of Sorrento* (1890)

The town on three sides is severed from the main land by a gorge two hundred feet in depth and forty or fifty in breadth, crossed by a bridge resting on double arches, the construction of which dates back to the time of the ancient Romans. This bridge affords a favorite lounging-place for the inhabitants, and at evening a motley assemblage may be seen lolling over its moss-grown sides, – men with their picturesque knit caps of scarlet or brown falling gracefully on one shoulder, and women with their shining black hair and the enormous pearl ear-rings which are the pride and heirlooms of every family. The present traveller at Sorrento may remember standing on this bridge and looking down the gloomy depths of the gorge, to where a fair villa, with its groves of orange-trees and gardens, overhangs the tremendous depths below.

...

... One could look down into the gloomy depths of the gorge, as into some mysterious underworld. Strange and weird it seemed, with its fathomless shadows and its wild grottoes, over which hung, silently waving, long pendants of ivy, while dusky gray aloes uplifted their horned heads from great rock-rifts, like elfin spirits struggling upward out of the shade. Nor was wanting the usual gentle poetry of flowers; for white iris leaned its fairy pavilion over the black void like a pale-cheeked princess from the window of some dark enchanted castle, and scarlet geranium and golden broom and crimson gladiolus waved and glowed in the shifting beams of the sunlight. Also there was in this little spot what forms the charm of Italian gardens always, – the sweet song and prattle of waters...

...

After her light supper was over, Agnes took her distaff, wound with shining white flax, and went and seated herself in her favorite place, on the low parapet that overlooked the gorge.

This ravine, with its dizzy depths, its waving foliage, its dripping springs, and the low murmur of the little stream that pursued its way far down at the bottom, was one of those things which stimulated her impressible imagination, and filled her with a solemn and vague delight. The

View of the Gorge (Valley of the Mills)

ancient Italian tradition made it the home of fauns and dryads, wild woodland creatures, intermediate links between vegetable life and that of sen-
tient and reasoning humanity. The more earnest faith that came in with
Christianity, if it had its brighter lights in an immortality of blessedness, had
also its deeper shadows in the intenser perceptions it awakened of sin and
evil, and of the mortal struggle by which the human spirit must avoid endless woe and rise to endless felicity...

Sites and Insights for the Visitor

*The topographical setting of Sorrento is quite extraordinary. Perched
on sheer tufa cliffs overhanging the sea, the town is also bounded by deep
gorges. Rivers running from the mountains to the sea carved two ravines
that terminate on the beaches of Marina Piccola and Marina Grande. Like
the cliffs, the gorges served a practical function for the Sorrentines by cre-
ating a natural and extremely steep moatlike defense to ward off invaders.
Today's visitor may be startled by the unsettling discovery that the
bustling center of town, Piazza Tasso, is built over one of these immense
gorges (known as the* Vallone dei Mulini) *leading to Marina Piccola.
Walking from Piazza Tasso along Via Fuori Mura, one can lean over a
railing to peer at the bottom of this gorge: wild, overgrown vegetation and
the crumbling remains of an old mill stir up nostalgic and sublime sensa-
tions of the passage of time.*

*From the turn-of-the-century descriptions above, one gets the distinct
impression that this gorge used to be much more accessible, fascinating
visitors with its inhabitants who domesticated its depths with orange trees
and flowers. Its former domesticity notwithstanding, foreign writers have
found the gorge a site of mystery and legends. Arthur H. Norway imag-
ines a secret treasure deep within the gorge, while Harriet Beecher Stowe
is reminded of "some mysterious underworld" occupied by pagan spirits
and woodland creatures. The gorge plays an important role in Stowe's
novel* Agnes of Sorrento (1890). *The author, primarily remembered for*
Uncle Tom's Cabin, *visited Sorrento in 1860 and was inspired to write a
novel when she saw some Sorrentine women near the gorge. As the physical setting for many scenes in the novel, the gorge also assumes a Christian dimension. In this American writer's moralized interpretation of the
landscape, the gorge seems symbolic of sin and evil and offers a foil to upper Sorrento which becomes a suitable setting for reflections on paradise.*

CHAPTER 4

SORRENTO OF THE SENSES

When Adam and Eve were expelled from Paradise, they lost the garden of our dreams. Perhaps visitors find a kind of substitute in Sorrento. Like all wonderful gardens, Sorrento offers not just its visual treats but also invitations to engage all our senses, sometimes several at once. In a journal entry written in 1937, Andrè Gide describes how from a distance Sorrento's ravines look like the fissures of a pomegranate heated to bursting by the sun. In that simile rich in sensual delight, Gide evokes the heavy leathery feel of the pomegranate, warmed by rays ripening it to the splitting point, the explosion of flavor as one's teeth crunch the jewel-like kernels filled with tangy juices. All this packed into a geological explanation! Here are further passages, by Gide during an earlier visit and by other observers, that pleasurably engage the senses.

ANDRÈ GIDE, *Journals* (1896)

Sorrento, Villa Arlotta; at Vollmoeller's

Who could describe the vividness, the somber magnificence, the order, the rhythmic beauty, the softness of this garden-orchard... I went in under the shade of the orange trees, half weeping, half laughing, and fully intoxicated; through the dense branches one could hardly see the sky. It had rained; the sky was still gray; it seemed that the light came entirely from the profusion of oranges... On the ground, among the trunks whose number, modest height, and oily and polished surface reminded me of the rich pillars in the Córdoba mosque, a thick, unbroken carpet of wood-sorrel of a paler green than lawns, more on the bluish side, more subtle, more fragile...

The garden ended in a terrace, or a cliff rather, dropping straight into the sea. On the extreme edge the orange grove yielded to ilex and pines... Where the rock jutted out, the bold terrace offered a circular bench, a table, a charming spot to rest. On one of these marble benches the diligent gardener had placed some oranges for our pleasure... the egg-shaped ones with a thick skin... had an ethereal taste such as I fancy Oriental oranges to have; but I especially delighted in the very small tangerines, hard as lady-apples, with an orangey-green skin of delicate texture that looks like a glove leather. I can't say how many we ate, nor yet, alas, with what rapture...

SYBIL FITZGERALD, *Naples* (1904)

... All is light and movement in the market... Rich masses of autumn fruits and vegetables are piled on the pavement in the square. When the red watermelons of summer are over, comes the season for the green and black figs, together with strings of tomatoes, baskets of the sweet *fravole-uva*, with its double flavour of grape and strawberry, and the gorgeous scarlet *peperoni*. All is massed up together, side by side with the colour of the medlars and that of the shining chestnuts...

HERBERT M. VAUGHAN, *The Naples Riviera* (1925)

... When the spring comes, here truly is a transformation from cold and torpor! The soft warm air is redolent of the penetrating fragrance of orange blossom, of stocks, of jessamine, of wallflower, and of a hundred odorous plants and shrubs from each garden and grove behind the many obstructing walls. The balconies and gate-pillars are draped in scented masses of the beautiful wistaria, which in Italy produces its long pendant bunches of purple flowers before putting forth its bronze-coloured leaves. Cascades of white and yellow banksia roses fall over each confining barrier, or else their stems may be seen climbing like huge serpents up the trunks of pine and olive, to burst forth amidst the topmost boughs into floral rockets against the cloudless sky. The ravines with which the whole of the Piano di Sorrento is intersected are filled with a perfect jungle of fresh spring foliage, amidst whose varied tints of green appear here and there the bright red shoots of the pomegranate trees bursting into leaf. In the heavily perfumed air at dusk, or when the bright moonlight is flooding the whole scene and is turning the Bay into a mirror of molten silver, the song of the innumerable nightingales can be heard resounding from all sides...

...

In early autumn also the place has its charms, in the days when the market is filled with stalls heaped with glowing masses of fruit, many of them unknown to us wanderers from the north. There are peaches that resemble our own fruit at home, and there are also great yellow flushed velvety globes, like the sun-kissed cheeks of a fair Sorrentina... There are hundreds of apples, some of a shining rich crimson and others of dull yellow pep-

Fresh fruit and vegetable stalls on Via San Cesareo

pered over with tiny black specks, the *renati*, highly prized by the natives for their delicate flavour and soft flesh. There are of course loads of grapes, varying from the little honey-tasting purple sort, that has been introduced from California, to the huge but somewhat insipid bunches of the white *Regina*; we note also the quaintly shaped "Ladies' Fingers," which are especially sweet. The figs, massed together in serried layers between fresh vine leaves and costing a *soldo* the dozen, stand around in glossy purple pyramids, so luscious that their sugary tears are exuding from their skins, and so ripe that they seem to cry to be eaten before noon. Here is a barrow piled high with the little green fruit, each separate fig being decorated with a pink cyclamen stuck in its crest; and here is a smaller load of the black *Vescovo*... No one who has not visited the shores of the Mediterranean in September or early October can realize the luscious possibilities of the fig; for there seems nothing in common between the freshly-picked fruit of the south, bursting its skin with liquid sugar, and the dry sweetish woolly object which tries to ripen on the sheltered wall of an English garden and is eaten with apparent gusto by those who know not its Italian brother. Being autumn, we have missed one prominent feature of the fruit market, the great green-skinned water-melons (*poponi*) with their rose-coloured pulp and masses of coal-black seeds, which form the favourite summer fruit of the people, who find both food and drink in their cool nutritious flesh. But even gayer and more striking than the fruits are the piles of vegetables, arranged with a fine appreciation of colour to which only an Italian eye can aspire. Carrots, turnips, tomatoes, purple-headed cauliflowers, all the broccoli and many others to be observed are old familiar friends, but who in England ever saw such gorgeous objects on a coster's stall or in a green-grocer's shop as the yellow, scarlet and shining green pods of the *peperoni*, or the banana-shaped egg-plants of iridescent purple, or the split pumpkins, revealing caverns of saffron-hued pulp within? Truly, the Sorrentine market contains a feast of colour to satisfy the craving of an artist!

At vintage time the whole Piano di Sorrento reeks with the vinous scent of the spilt juice, that is carelessly thrown on to the stone-paved roads by the jolting of the country carts which bring in the great wooden tubs, so that the very streets seem to run with the crimson ooze. Slender youths in yet more slender clothing, with legs purple-stained from treading the grapes (for in the South wine is still made on the primitive plan), are to be met with on all sides, playing at their favourite game of bowls on the public road, in order to relieve their brains of the pungent fumes of the fermenting grape juice. Somehow at the very thought of a Campanian vintage with its long hot dusty days, its bare-legged brown-skinned peasants treading the pulp, and its all-pervading aroma of wine-lees, there rise to memory the truly inspired lines of John Keats:

"O for a draught of vintage, that hath been
Cool'd a long age in the deep-delved earth,
Tasting of Flora and the country-green,
Dance, and Provençal song, and sun-burnt mirth!
O for a beaker full of the warm South,
Full of the true, the blushful Hippocrene,
With beaded bubbles winking at the brim,
And purple-stained mouth."

* * *

The noted English poet Robert Browning frequently visited Italy, but he composed only a single work about his experience of southern Italy, the poem below, "An Englishman in Italy." Nor did he often write with such sensual description as in this poem. The work was probably composed soon after he wandered the plain of Sorrento in the autumn of 1844. Elizabeth Barrett, who became his wife, may have encouraged

Refreshments in Piazza Tasso

him to expand his lusciously evocative poem by adding a political "moral" in the last seven lines. Elizabeth Barrett liked the addition; she felt it gave the poem unity. For a modern reader, Browning's ending falls a bit short. Yes, clearly the world would be a better place without scirocco – that deadly south wind, just as England would have been a better country without Corn Laws protecting the rich by starving the poor. But scirocco is a given of nature, and so too seems the human greed that produces Corn Laws in every century under whatever name. Not for the political argument do we read this poem today, but for its rich sensuous descriptions. The poem may seem difficult at first, but on leisurely reading (and re-reading) it proves a savory delight.

ROBERT BROWNING, "The Englishman in Italy - Piano di Sorrento" (1845)

Fortù, Fortù, my beloved one,
    Sit here by my side,
On my knees put up both little feet!
    I was sure, if I tried,
I could make you laugh spite of Scirocco.
    Now, open your eyes,
Let me keep you amused till he vanish
    In black from the skies,
With telling my memories over
    As you tell your beads;
All the Plain saw me gather, I garland
    – The flowers or the weeds.

Time for rain! for your long hot dry Autumn
    Had net-worked with brown
The white skin of each grape on the bunches,
    Marked like a quail's crown,
Those creatures you make such account of,
    Whose heads, – speckled white
Over brown like a great spider's back,
    As I told you last night, –
Your mother bites off for her supper.
    Red-ripe as could be,
Pomegranates were chapping and splitting
    In halves on the tree:

And betwixt the loose walls of great flintstone,
    Or in the thick dust
On the path, or straight out of the rock-side,
    Wherever could thrust
Some burnt sprig of bold hardy rock-flower
    Its yellow face up,
For the prize were great butterflies fighting,
    Some five for one cup.
So, I guessed, ere I got up this morning,
    What change was in store,
By the quick rustle-down of the quail-nets
    Which woke me before
I could open my shutter, made fast
    With a bough and a stone,
And look thro' the twisted dead vine-twigs,
    Sole lattice that's known.
Quick and sharp rang the rings down the net-poles,
    While, busy beneath,
Your priest and his brother tugged at them,
    The rain in their teeth.
And out upon all the flat house-roofs
    Where split figs lay drying
The girls took the frails under cover:
    Nor use seemed in trying
To get out the boats and go fishing,
    For, under the cliff,
Fierce the black water frothed o'er the blind-rock.
    No seeing our skiff
Arrive about noon from Amalfi,
    – Our fisher arrive,
And pitch down his basket before us,
    All trembling alive
With pink and grey jellies, your sea-fruit;
    You touch the strange lumps,
And mouths gape there, eyes open, all manner
    Of horns and of humps,
Which only the fisher looks grave at,
    While round him like imps
Cling screaming the children as naked
    And brown as his shrimps:

Himself too as bare to the middle
   – You see round his neck
The string and its brass coin suspended,
   That saves him from wreck.
But to-day not a boat reached Salerno
   So back, to a man,
Came our friends, with whose help in the vineyards
   Grape-harvest began.
In the vat, halfway up in our house-side,
   Like blood the juice spins,
While your brother all bare-legged is dancing
   Till breathless he grins
Dead-beaten in effort on effort
   To keep the grapes under,
Since still when he seems all but master,
   In pours the fresh plunder
From girls who keep coming and going
   With basket on shoulder,
And eyes shut against the rain's driving;
   Your girls that are older, –
For under the hedges of aloe,
   And where, on its bed
Of the orchard's black mould, the love-apple
   Lies pulpy and red,
All the young ones are kneeling and filling
   Their laps with the snails
Tempted out by this first rainy weather, –
   Your best of regales,
As to-night will be proved to my sorrow,
   When, supping in state,
We shall feast our grape-gleaners (two dozen,
   Three over one plate)
With lasagne so tempting to swallow
   In slippery ropes
And gourds fried in great purple slices,
   That colour of popes.
Meantime, see the grape bunch they've brought you:
   The rain-water slips
O'er the heavy blue bloom on each globe
   Which the wasp to your lips

Still follows with fretful persistence:
  Nay, taste, while awake,
This half of a curd-white smooth cheese-ball
  That peels, flake by flake,
Like an onion, each smoother and whiter;
  Next, sip this weak wine
From the thin green glass flask, with its stopper,
  A leaf of the vine;
And end with the prickly-pear's red flesh
  That leaves thro' its juice
The stony black seeds on your pearl-teeth.
  Scirocco is loose!
Hark, the quick, whistling pelt of the olives
  Which, thick in one's track,
Tempt the stranger to pick up and bite them,
  Tho' not yet half black!
How the old twisted olive trunks shudder,
  The medlars let fall
Their hard fruit, and the brittle great fig-trees
  Snap off, figs and all,
For here comes the whole of the tempest!
  No refuge, but creep
Back again to my side and my shoulder,
  And listen or sleep.

O how will your country show next week,
  When all the vine-boughs
Have been stripped of their foliage to pasture
  The mules and the cows?
Last eve, I rode over the mountains;
  Your brother, my guide,
Soon left me, to feast on the myrtles
  That offered, each side,
Their fruit-balls, black, glossy and luscious, –
  Or strip from the sorbs
A treasure, or, rosy and wondrous,
  Those hairy gold orbs!
But my mule picked his sure sober path out,
  Just stopping to neigh
When he recognized down in the valley
  His mates on their way

With the faggots and barrels of water;
    And soon we emerged
From the plain, where the woods could scarce follow;
    And still as we urged
Our way, the woods wondered, and left us,
    As up still we trudged
Though the wild path grew wilder each instant,
    And place was e'en grudged
'Mid the rock-chasms and piles of loose stones
    Like the loose broken teeth
Of some monster which climbed there to die
    From the ocean beneath –
Place was grudged to the silver-grey fume-weed
    That clung to the path,
And dark rosemary ever a-dying
    That, 'spite the wind's wrath,
So loves the salt rock's face to seaward,
    And lentisks as staunch
To the stone where they root and bear berries,
    And... what shows a branch
Coral-coloured, transparent, with circlets
    Of pale seagreen leaves;
Over all trod my mule with the caution
    Of gleaners o'er sheaves,
Still, foot after foot like a lady,
    Till, round after round,
He climbed to the top of Calvano,
    And God's own profound
Was above me, and round me the mountains,
    And under, the sea,
And within me my heart to bear witness
    What was and shall be.
Oh, heaven and the terrible crystal!
    No rampart excludes
Your eye from the life to be lived
    In the blue solitudes.
Oh, those mountains, their infinite movement!
    Still moving with you;
For, ever some new head and breast of them
    Thrusts into view

To observe the intruder; you see it
    If quickly you turn
And, before they escape you surprise them.
    They grudge you should learn
How the soft plains they look on, lean over
    And love (they pretend)
– Cower beneath them, the flat sea-pine crouches,
    The wild fruit-trees bend,
E'en the myrtle-leaves curl, shrink and shut:
    All is silent and grave:
'T is a sensual and timorous beauty,
    How fair! but a slave.
So, I turned to the sea; and there slumbered
    As greenly as ever
Those isles of the siren, your Galli;
    No ages can sever
The Three, nor enable their sister
    To join them, – halfway
On the voyage, she looked at Ulysses –
    No farther to-day,
Tho' the small one, just launched in the wave,
    Watches, breast-high and steady
From under the rock, her bold sister
    Swum halfway already.
Fortù, shall we sail there together
    And see from the sides
Quite new rocks show their faces, new haunts
    Where the siren abides?
Shall we sail round and round them, close over
    The rocks, tho' unseen,
That ruffle the grey glassy water
    To glorious green?
Then scramble from splinter to splinter,
    Reach land and explore,
On the largest, the strange square black turret
    With never a door,
Just a loop to admit the quick lizards;
    Then, stand there and hear
The birds' quiet singing, that tells us
    What life is, so clear?

– The secret they sang to Ulysses
    When, ages ago,
He heard and he knew this life's secret
    I hear and I know.

Ah, see! the sun breaks o'er Calvano;
    He strikes the great gloom
And flutters it o'er the mount's summit
    In airy gold fume.
All is over. Look out, see the gipsy,
    Our tinker and smith,
Has arrived, set up bellows and forge,
    And down-squatted forthwith
To his hammering, under the wall there;
    One eye keeps aloof
The urchins that itch to be putting
    His jews'-harps to proof,
While the other, thro' locks of curled wire,
    Is watching how sleek
Shines the hog, come to share in the windfall
    – Chew, abbot's own cheek!
All is over. Wake up and come out now,
    And down let us go,
And see the fine things got in order
    At church for the show
Of the Sacrament, set forth this evening.
    To-morrow's the Feast
Of the Rosary's Virgin, by no means
    Of Virgins the least,
As you'll hear in the oft-hand discourse
    Which (all nature, no art)
The Dominican brother, these three weeks,
    Was getting by heart.
Not a pillar nor post but is dizened
    With red and blue papers;
All the roof waves with ribbons, each altar
    A-blaze with long tapers;
But the great masterpiece is the scaffold
    Rigged glorious to hold
All the fiddlers and fifers and drummers
    And trumpters bold,

Not afraid of Bellini nor Auber,
    Who, when the priest's hoarse,
Will strike us up something that's brisk
    For the feast's second course.
And then will the flaxen-wigged Image
    Be carried in pomp
Thro' the plain, while in gallant procession
    The priests mean to stomp.
All round the glad church lie old bottles
    With gunpowder stopped,
Which will be, when the Image re-enters,
    Religiously popped;
And at night from the crest of Calvano
    Great bonfires will hang,
On the plain will the trumpets join chorus,
    And more poppers bang.
At all events, come – to the garden
    As far as the wall;
See me tap with a hoe on the plaster
    Till out there shall fall
A scorpion with wide angry nippers!

    – "Such trifles!" you say?
Fortù, in my England at home,
    Men meet gravely to-day
And debate, if abolishing Corn-laws
    Be righteous and wise
– If 't were proper, Scirocco should vanish
    In black from the skies!

CHAPTER 5

THE SORRENTINES
AND THEIR CUSTOMS

The visitors whose writings appear in this chapter lived in Sorrento for short periods of time. Their visits took place over seventy-five years, from the late 1850s to the mid-1920s. They made observations about the inhabitants, their social structure, and the place of religion in their lives. These writers' recollections, whether published as fiction or non-fiction, are literary; none of them was trained as, or professes to be, a sociologist.

These visitors came to Sorrento for a variety reasons. Some were here to seek a quiet place to do their literary work in a serene and beautiful environment. Some were here to write about Sorrento specifically. Some were here to experience the *dolce far niente* for which the area is known. Some were here for reasons which are unstated or are forgotten.

Because they were written by foreigners, these observations are laden with concepts from the visitors' own cultures. They interpret what they see by a frame of reference which is British or American or French. In such circumstances it is difficult to avoid remarking on superficial likenesses and differences. Still, many of the accounts are humorous, or are keen, and, perhaps, give insight into Sorrentine life at the time.

The People and Their Commerce

The selections which follow note the physical appearance of the people, the markets filled with fruits of the earth (especially lemons and oranges) and the fruits of the labor of artisans, made from olive wood and silk. Julia Kavanagh's account, concluding this section, places the fruits and crafts in context by describing the family unit, working together in the production of these goods.

HARRIET BEECHER STOWE, *Agnes of Sorrento* (1890)

... Under all these cherishing influences, the human being develops a wealth and luxuriance of physical beauty unknown in less favored regions. In the region about Sorrento one may be said to have found the land where beauty is the rule and not the exception. The singularity there is not to see handsome points of physical proportion, but rather to see those who are without them. Scarce a man, woman, or child you meet who has not some personal advantage to be commended, while even striking beauty is common. Also, under these kindly skies, a native courtesy and gentleness of manner make themselves felt. It would seem as if humanity, rocked in this flowery cradle, and soothed by so many daily caresses and appliances of nursing Nature, grew up with all that is kindliest on the outward, – not repressed and beat in, as under the inclement atmosphere and stormy skies of the North.

SYBIL FITZGERALD, *Naples* (1904)

The most casual stranger who lingers at Sorrento must remark the great difference between the character of the Sorrentian and that of the Neapolitan. There is I know not what of primitiveness and naïveté about the Sorrentians. By this I mean, not that they are less practical or less interested, but that the traditional simplicity of a fisher population contrasts with the intellectual corruption of the over-sophisticated Neapolitan. This is a trait noticeable more or less in all the little fishing towns along the coast. The fisher-folks are robust and honest, fine types of healthy and hard-working men. They have, moreover, a strong individuality of their own, and a delicate, if intricate, sense of humour, all the more remarkable because humour plays so slight a part in the Italian character. The fact that this little population can intermarry almost entirely among themselves for so many generations, and produce such splendid types of physique, is a striking proof of their vitality. The deformities which fill the little towns of Italy produce here only a quaint stunted growth, still healthy and strong, human gargoyles with a dignity of their own, like the dwarfs of Velasquez. The women, too, may be said to be even stronger than the men. The work they do is often harder than that done by men – and that in spite of the enormous families they rear. Women, young and quite old, may be seen toiling along the road to Sorrento beneath burdens which even a Northern labourer would hesitate to fasten upon his back. They wear short petticoats, showing their bare legs, and feet bound with twisted rags to steady the ankles – a strange sight at first. They say "Buon giorno" light-heartedly

Fisherman repairing nets at Marina Grande

as we pass them, and the sturdy simplicity of their lives is such that the problems which preoccupy us do not exist for them.

...

... Go into the market-place in the morning, and you will find a spectacle that cannot be surpassed for picturesque charm. Part of this piazza is built over the great gorge beginning in the hills and descending rapidly to the sea, and once a roaring torrent must have dashed down the ravine. The line of the old town wall of medieval times which once followed it has now disappeared and has given place to a fine road. Crumbling ruins are incongruous in Sorrento, and the hand of man has not been idle in helping to remove them. On one side of the Piazza the bright plaster facade of a little rococo church and the pink and yellow houses glitter in the sun. A splendid sweep of hills forms the background of this picture. In colour these hills behind Sorrento run to the deepest blue, and in the early morning mists great wreaths of clouds hang about them delightfully, now hiding, now revealing some distant habitation or rugged mountain precipice; or, again, some wild garden of olives and dim tufa rocks. On the other side the sea gleams through the steep defile of precipitous rock overgrown with the most lovely wilderness of creepers, which here run sheer down to the shore. All is light and movement in the market. Mules with shining brass ornaments, and harness which is literally made up of charms and prophy-lactics, are descending from the hills, down the mountain paths. Rich masses of autumn fruits and vegetables are piled on the pavement in the square. When the red watermelons of summer are over, comes the season for the green and black figs, together with strings of tomatoes, baskets of the sweet *fravole-uva*, with its double flavour of grape and strawberry, and the gorgeous scarlet *peperoni*. All is massed up together, side by side with the colour of the medlars and that of the shining chestnuts. Eager groups of buyers and sellers are chattering over their merchandise. Oh, this eternal bargaining of the South! What a zest it gives to the daily routine of life! I saw a small boy, certainly not more than ten years of age, trying to sell some half-dozen coloured handkerchiefs to the girls about the place. Each girl seized one of the gaudy fichus of cotton, shook it out of its neat folds, tossed it from hand to hand among her companions with critical remarks, and finally offered him three of the six soldi he had asked. The poor little wretch could not come down in his price on his own responsibility, and af-ter twenty minutes of useless haggling the dishevelled handkerchiefs were thrown back to him contemptuously. During the scene the girls were munching at enormous loaves of bread, which they held under one arm, tearing pieces off. At the height of the bargaining a big boy was busily de-vouring the loaf from behind the arm of one of the haggling girls. I felt quite sorry for the urchin, who looked both hungry and unspeakably weary of feminine society; but no doubt these are the early struggles that form the character of manhood.

Quarrels are rare here; but when they do occur the vociferation is end-less, and the whole Piazza stands round and watches with interest. A veri-table chorus of Aristophanes.

HERBERT M. VAUGHAN, *The Naples Riviera* (1925)

... One of the chief industries of the place is the manufacture of scarves and sashes of rich silk woven in cross bars of strong contrasting colours, so that the Sorrentine silk work strongly resembles the well-known Roman va-riety. Equally popular with visitors are the various articles made of olive wood and decorated in *tarsia*, the art of inlaying with pieces of stained wood, which is a speciality of the place. There are two kinds of this Sor-rentine inlaid work; one consisting of figures of peasants dancing the *taran-tella*, of Pompeian maidens in classical drapery, of *contadini* or priests bestriding mules, and of similar local subjects; and the other, of fanciful patterns made up of tiny coloured cubes of wood, much in the style of the old Roman stone mosaics. The designs employed vary of course with the fashion of the day, for there is a local school of art supported by the municipality, which professes to improve the tastes of the *tarsiatori,* but most persons will certainly prefer the trite but characteristic patterns of the place.

But the main industry of Sorrento consists in the culture of the orange; and the dark groves, covered with their globes of shining yellow fruit, "like golden lamps in a green light," to quote Andrew Marvell's charming conceit, constitute the chief feature of its environs. Even the coat-of-arms of the medieval city, showing a golden crown encircled by a wreath of the dark glossy leaves, attests the antiquity of this industry here. The cultivation of the orange in Southern Italy is by no means an easy pursuit, though under favourable conditions it may prove a very lucrative one, even in a spot so subject to sudden changes of temperature as Sorrento in winter time, when a continuance of severe weather, like that experienced around Naples in the opening months of the year 1905, means total destruction of the fruit crop and temporary ruin to the owners.

The fruit of commerce is propagated by means of grafting the sweet variety on to the stock of the bitter orange – said on doubtful authority to be indigenous to this district – which is fairly hardy and can be grown in the open as far north as Tuscany, so that every *aranciaria* ought to possess a nursery of flourishing young sweet-orange shoots, ready in case of necessity. For eight long years the grafted tree remains as a rule profitless, but having survived and thriven so long, it then becomes a valuable asset to its proprietor for an indefinite period; – as a proof of the longevity of the orange under normal conditions we may cite the famous tree in a Roman convent garden, which on good authority is stated to have been planted by St Dominic nearly six hundred years ago. As to the amount of fruit yielded, the growers of Sorrento commonly aver that one good year, one bad year and one mediocre year constitute the general cycle in the prospects of orange farming. Two crops are gathered annually, the principle one in December and the other at Eastertide, the fruit produced by the later and smaller crop being far finer in size and flavour than those of the Christmas harvest. Mandarin oranges are gathered on both occasions, but the large luscious loose-skinned fruit of March and April – *Portogalli* as they are commonly termed – are far superior to the small hard specimens that appear in December, and seem to consist of little else than rind, scent and seeds. The oranges begin to form in spring time, almost before the petals have fallen, when the peasants anxiously draw their conclusions as to the expected yield. But however valuable the fruit, the wood of the tree is worthless for commerce, except to make walking-sticks, or to serve the ignoble purpose of supplying hotels and cafés with tooth-picks! Lemons, which are far more delicate than oranges and require to be kept protected by screens and matting during the sharp winter nights, are less common at Sorrento than on the warmer shores of the Bay of Baia or the sunny terraced slopes of the Amalfitan coast.

Julia Kavanagh, *A Summer and Winter in the Two Sicilies* (1858)

Carmela has just appeared on the little flat loggia that crowns her father's house. The free and happy girl, so shy in her liberty, and who though but a peasant, claims to be of the same race with a saint and a bishop, may also be a daughter of Spartacus, a descendant of the ancient bondsmen and bondwomen of the land. Of this she certainly never thinks, and I am not sure that the real meaning of the sad word "slave" has ever reached her. She may look at Vesuvius for ever, and never guess that it possesses records as sad as those of the eruptions which she thinks so terrible. The past for her is but another present, remote and indistinct, but essentially the same.

She is just now very busy; a square blue handkerchief is folded on her head to protect her from the hot noonday sun; thus sheltered she opens figs and spreads them out to dry for the winter's provisions; but in the midst of her task she sees me and gives me a gentle bend of her head and a little wave of her hand, of which an English duchess might envy the easy grace.

...

Since Carmela has thus come across me, I cannot do better than describe her, her mode of life, and at the same time give the reader some knowledge of the ways of an Italian farm, or masseria.

Carmela is twenty-three, molto vecchia, very old, as she says herself with demure gravity. She is neither tall nor short, but slender in figure, light and agile as a deer, and, above all, graceful from the bend of her slim arched neck to the springing step of her bare brown feet. She wears her black hair in the becoming Greek fashion, which, two thousand years ago, her Greek ancestresses brought with them to Sorrento. That is to say, she divides it at the back into two plaits, with which she braids her head like a crown; two ends of black ribbon and a long silver bodkin which they call spadella from its sword-like shape, fasten these plaits securely behind, the rest of her attire offers nothing striking; a cotton handkerchief around her neck, white linen sleeves tucked up to her elbow, a short-waisted little boddice, a long skirt and a wide apron complete her toilet. Like her father, mother, brothers and sisters, Carmela wears neither shoes nor stockings. They are comfortable people; they have cows and pigs, and hens and silkworms, and a good farm of orange, lemon, and olive trees, but they would think it a strange luxury to wear shoes and stockings on week-days or in summer. It is only in winter, or on Sundays and holy days, that the whole family is duly shod.

Carmela is not strictly beautiful, but she is better than pretty; delightful is the only word that will describe her. Her features are arched and expressive; her brown eyes have the look, soft and wild, of a young kid. There is mischief in the very sweetness of her smile, but maiden mischief securely guarded round by maiden innocence. Carmela is guarded too by that other good angel of youth – active life. Early as I may get up, I see the tremulous blue smoke rising from her father's chimney amongst the olive and orange trees, and we rarely go to bed but we leave a light burning in Carmela's windows and hear the whole family saying the rosary; work, and hard work, fills the interval. Except on Sundays and Festas this family, seven in all, are never a moment idle.

...

A large garden surrounds the old farm-house. I shall never forget my feeling of delight when I first entered this Italian orchard, the first of its kind that I had yet seen. A narrow path shaded by olives, some of which had reached the size and strength of oaks, and which had been planted there to shield the orange-trees against the winter winds, wound by the side of the sea. No wall rose here; the steep cliffs sufficiently guarded the place; and the whole of the broad blue bay from Ischia to Vesuvius lay below us. Another path led us into the orange-groves; taller and stronger than pear-trees they grew, and thicker than apples hung the oranges on their boughs; their brilliant foliage was so dense and their branches were so close that the sun could not pierce them; only here and there a ray glided in through the green gloom, and lit a cluster of oranges on its way. Six and seven in a bunch some grew; others were scattered on the rich red earth, and lay there at the foot of the trees like things uncared for. Wherever we turned we saw the glorious Hesperian fruit shining before us, and I thought I had never seen anything so splendid.

This house and garden keep the whole family in constant occupation; the men dig the earth, and in every available spot sow potatoes, beans, peas, and pumpkins for home consumption. The women mind the house, the cows, the hens, and rear the silk-worms.

...

Silk is another source of income in this favoured country. The rearing of silkworms – a delicate task, requiring constant care – is left to women. In the month of May they take the seed [chrysalis], wrap it in a fine linen cloth, and place it in their beds when they rise in the morning. This degree of animal heat is sufficient; but every door and window must be kept securely closed, lest a chill breath of air should reach this dainty treasure, which, in the cheapest years, costs a ducat an ounce, and which, this season, rose to four. When the seed is hatched, the young worms are placed in a flat basket, lined with the youngest and most tender of mulberry leaves. These require to be renewed day and night. The worms are never touched; the leaves are merely placed above them; they seize on them voraciously. The quantity they devour and the noise they make in eating are astonishing. It is a curious sight to see whole rooms filled with these baskets, with the yellowish white worms crawling on their green leaves, and raising and stretching their heads in search of food.

When the worm is full sized, it is fed no more. The women take it away from the basket, and having ascertained, by drawing it backwards, that the silk issues from its mouth, they place it on a dry twig; there it is to weave the mysterious home in which its being is transformed. These little creatures take a long time to make up their minds – they wander restlessly from point to point of their twig, they stretch their heads, they turn round, they remain quiet, they move again, at length they begin. First of all, they throw around them a fine white silk, which is the sort of down in which the chrysalis is enveloped; then, within that, they weave their shroud of pure white or shining yellow. Round and round turn the unwearied little labourers, two sometimes unite, drawing the silk from their mouth with their tiny claws, and working it with mingled ardour and patience. Less and less distinct they become, until the last dim outline of their diminished body has vanished. But their task is not over yet – the outer garment is fashioned, it must be lined. It is only when their stock of silk is exhausted that they know their labour to be perfect; then, wearied and exhausted, they cease and sleep until the day of the wakening. For some, alas! that day never comes. They are taken in their helpless state, and baked in an oven, or roasted in the hot noonday sun. At the end of Carmela's garden, close by the olive path on the edge of the cliff that seems to hang above the sea, there is a rude stone furnace, black with smoke, where their fate is consummated; for in the top of that furnace there is a hollow in which an iron cauldron fits; and in the month of August, when the two crops of silk are in – the second begins in June – men come, light the fire in the furnace, put on the cauldron full of water, and, when it boils, throw in the baked and roasted cocoons. The boiling water loosens the silk; with great dexterity the men catch up the flying threads, and throw them on a large reel close by. Swift it turns, with a buzzing sound, unwinding the beautiful glossy silk, whilst the poor black chrysalidae, like mummies in their swathings, cover the ground. But nothing must be wasted; they are gathered, and sold to bird-fanciers in Naples. Certain outlandish birds, of which I have not been able to ascertain the name, feed on this dainty, whilst the shining spoils of the victim travel all over the world to adorn the beauties of every land.

Their Sense of Charity

The practice of begging is duly noted by foreign visitors. They tend to find the practice less aggressive in Sorrento than in other locations; they also note charitable practices among the Sorrentines.

SYBIL FITZGERALD, *Naples* (1904)

> Perhaps the Sorrentians occasionally trade somewhat on the stranger's belief in their native simplicity, and seem at times to realise that a little cunning among a sleepy people is refreshing to others. But the people of this *paese* are still far above the degradation of the dishonesty in Naples, where nothing is ever done except for money. An offer there to do anything "for love" must be distrusted – as when that Company who offered to build a home for the Little Sisters of the Poor (to all appearance so reasonably that it seemed, as they said, "per amore de Dio") built it entirely without foundations. Unfortunately, there is a begging population here – large for so small and so prosperous a place. Rosy-cheeked and healthy children, and even well-dressed peasants, will beg audaciously. Beggars infest all this coast. The tourist evidently does not believe that it is better that "the lazy should die of hunger than be fed in idleness." The Greek and Egyptian spirit in which idleness was deserving of death would quite upset the modern travellers' delight in flinging coppers into the dust and watching their poorer brethren scramble for them.

AUGUSTUS J. C. HARE, *Cities of Southern Italy and Sicily* (1891)

> The people of Sorrento are for the most part unspoiled, and civil to strangers. The women wear pretty blue lace veils on festas, and the processions at Christmas and on Good Friday and several church festivals are striking and picturesque. If you give to beggars, they thank you with "La Madonna v'accompagna," or "Cento mill' anni," meaning "May you have a hundred thousand years' freedom from purgatory." The dialect, however, is harsh and very unpleasant...

JULIA KAVANAGH, *A Summer and Winter in the Two Sicilies* (1858)

... Has anyone ever studied attentively Italian charity? Not mere alms-giving, but love of the poor, – but a gentleness and a forbearance they rarely find elsewhere. Most travellers complain of the persecutions they endure from Italian beggars...

...

... The door of Carmela's home is besieged by beggars; they knock at it with lamentable petitions the whole day long. It rarely remains closed upon them, and more rarely opens to give them a denial. Still it sometimes happens that there are no fallen oranges, no remains of the noonday meal to bestow, but the ungracious "there is nothing for you," is never uttered by Carmela. "Have patience," she says, gently, and with more regret in her look and tone than the beggar whom she dismisses.

This is the common form of charity; but there is a form of charity which, without being peculiar to the kingdom of Naples, prevails in it to a great extent; the adoption of children by the poor. A few years ago, a foreigner entered the house of a poor Neapolitan woman, and found, what is common enough in that populous country, a houseful of children.

"Are they all yours?" he asked.

"All save these two," she replied. "They are children of the Madonna."

Which meant, that having lost two of her own children, the poor woman, in violation of all the sound principles of political economy, had picked up these two little strangers, and replaced her dead darlings by the offspring, for all she knew of vice and crime.

But thus do not reason the ignorant poor of Naples. They do not trouble themselves about the earthly parents these children may have had. The purest of virgins, the mildest of mothers, is the mother of the forsaken ones; they are the very children of God, the very brothers and sisters of Christ, and it must not be supposed that these children are not as kindly treated, as tenderly loved, as if they were the flesh and blood of their adoptive parents.

Their Legends and Folklore

The reported legends tend to reinforce a view of the people of Sorrento as being simple, unsophisticated and superstitious. They make for interesting accounts, but probably are heavily influenced by the natural inclination of foreigners to note the differences from the folklore of their own culture. Certain legends reflect the importance of religious beliefs among the people as well as the linking of these beliefs to other cultural elements.

HERBERT M. VAUGHAN, *The Naples Riviera* (1925)

On a modest scale Sorrento can lay claim to be called an eternal city, for the Surrentum of the ancient Romans was a place of no small importance, filled with villas of wealthy citizens and boasting a fair-sized population, as its numerous remains of antiquity can easily testify; whilst its crumbling ivy-clad walls and towers point to its prosperity during the Middle Ages, when Sorrento shared the political fortunes of Naples. It is now a busy thriving little cathedral town, and the possessor of silk and *tarsia* work industries, so that like Imperial Rome it can boast a continuous existence as a city from remote times to the present day. Its chief local Saint – for what Italian town does not boast a special patron? – is Sant' Antonio, whose most famous feat is said to have been the administering of a severe drubbing to Sicardo, Duke of Benevento, for daring to interfere with the liberties of his city in the ninth century. It would appear from the legend that all arguments as to ancient rights, the quality of mercy and the honour of keeping faith having been vainly exhausted upon the cruel and obstinate prince, Bishop Antonio came forward with a stout cudgel and belaboured the tyrant in order to obtain a favourable answer to the people's petition. The sanctity of the pugnacious prelate and the force of this *argumentum ad baculum* were evidently too much for the Duke of Benevento, who at once conceded the popular demands, whilst Antonio's name has deservedly descended to posterity as the capable protector of his native city.

ARTHUR H. NORWAY, *Naples, Past and Present* (1901)

There can, I think, be few districts in which the folklore is richer or more romantic than in this region of Sorrento. The peasants are soaked in superstition. The higher classes are scarce more free from it. Those who loiter at midnight near the Capo di Sorrento, whither every tourist goes to see the ruins of the Villa Pollio and the great cool reservoir of sea-water known as "Il Bagno della Regina Giovanna," may see a maiden clad in white robes rise out of the sea and glide over the water towards the Marina di Puolo, the little beach which lies between the Punta della Calcerella and the Portiglione. She has scarce touched land when she is pursued by a dark rider on a winged horse, who comes from the direction of Sorrento, and hunts her shrieking all along the shore. There are spectres on every cliff and hillside, witches on the way to their unhallowed gatherings at Benevento, and wizards prowling up and down in the shape of goats or dogs. At night the peasants keep their doors and windows closed; if they do not, the Janara may come in and cripple the babies. You may sometimes keep out evil spirits by setting a basin full of water near the door; the fiends will stop to count the drops, which takes a long time, probably enough to occupy them until day drives them home.

If anyone be out after dark it is better not to look round. The risk is that one may be turned into stone.

Here and there one may see ruined churches in the country, but no peasant will go near them after nightfall; for he knows that spectral Masses are celebrated there, solemn services chanted by dead priests, who are thus punished for neglect of their offices in life, and whose congregation is made up of worshippers who forgot their religion while they lived.

The Italian fancy begets things terrible more easily than it conceives a lovely dream. Even the tales of fairies turn more readily on fear than on the merry pranks with which our northern legends associate the dwellers in the foxglove bells. But on a fine spring evening, when the sun is glowing over the plain, there are pleasanter things to think of in Sorrento than the spirits of the other world. I turn gladly away from the ravines into the broad main street, and passing by the cathedral, pause in the piazza, where the life of the pleasant little town is busiest and gayest. It is here that one should call to mind the poet Tasso, whose tragedy was cast into noble verse by Goethe; for his statue stands in the square, looking down gravely on the rows of vetturini cracking whips, the children coming or going to the fountain, the babble of strange tongues from lands which never dreamt of Surriento when he dwelt on earth. But I think the days are gone in which English people can delight in the sixteenth-century poets of which Italy was once so proud. Tasso and Ariosto may have every merit save sincerity; but that is lacking, and Italy has so many noble poets who possess it! I care little for the memories of Tasso, save in Goethe's verse, and as I go down to the Marina it is of older visitors, welcome and unwelcome, that my mind is full – St. Peter, for example. There is a constant legend that he came this way after the death of Christ, landing perhaps from some galley of Alexandria that touched here on its way to Pozzuoli, and set down the apostle to win what souls he could among the rough dwellers in the mountains. The saint preached his first sermon by the roadside near Sant'Agnello, a village between Sorrento and the Marina di Cassano; and then went over the hills towards Castellammare, where he rewarded the hospitality of the dwellers at Mojano, near the roots of Faito, by making springs of water gush out of the thirsty rock.

Doubtless the apostle was on his way to Rome. I know no reason why we should distrust the tale that he did indeed pass through this country. The water way from the East around the coasts of southern Italy is of mysterious antiquity. Paestum was a mighty trading city many centuries before St. Peter lived, and its sailors may well have inherited traditions of navigation as much older than their day as they are older than our own. I do not know whether it was indeed upon the islands under the Punta di Campanella that Ulysses, lashed to the mast, heard the singing of the Sirens, but the tradition is not doubted in Sorrento; and without leaning on it as a fact, one may recognise at least that the tale suggests the vast antiquity of trade upon these waters. Else whence came the heaps of whitening bones of lost sailors, among which the Sirens sat and sang? Here year by year we learn more of the age of man, and of the countless centuries he has dwelt by the shore of the great deep. We cannot tell when he first adventured round the promontories with sail and oar; but it is safe to believe that those early voyages were made unnumbered centuries before any people lived whose records have come down to us, and that those sailors whom we discern when the mists are first lifted from the face of history were no pioneers, but followed in a well-worn track of trade, beaten out who knows how long before their time.

Their Social Structure

The foreign visitors, in varying degrees, experience some exclusion from the society of Sorrento. W. J. A. Stamer claims "there is absolutely no society." Having come to spend a summer of *dolce far niente*, he describes his daily routine: arise at six and write until eight; bathe in the nearby grotto at eight to avoid the presence of the local bathers; breakfast at noon; siesta, followed by conversations with the owners of the villa from which he is renting rooms or with a single neighbor who has a "tasteful garden" with a "Norfolk Island pine"; dinner at six, frequently followed by an evening of conversation with the Archdeacon of Sorrento, who has visited England and loves to draw comparisons between England and Italy. Such a schedule is not likely to reveal the complexities of the local social structure.

Julia Kavanagh spent part of her childhood in France, gaining insight into French life. Having had the experience of living in a culture other than that of her native Ireland, she seems to be more successful in crossing some, though certainly not all, of the barriers to Sorrentine social life. She has made friends with the family of Carmela, whose life she described in passages earlier, and the family entrusts her to take Carmela on *passeggiate* on the water – sometimes nearby, coasting by Villa Pollio, and once as far as Capri. She is invited to converse with countesses and is included in religious celebrations. It is relevant that her residence spans more than one season. She arrives in May and does not depart until the following March.

W. J. A. STAMER, *Dolce Napoli* (1878)

Lest the reader should imagine, from the above description of my daily life, that Sorrento must be the most desirable residence in all creation, I had better show the reverse side of the picture – state what are the drawbacks to one's perfect felicity and contentment.

Imprimis, there is absolutely no society; not a family is there in the entire *piano* that can be said to receive. Until the fall of the Bourbons Sorrento was a fashionable summer resort. The Counts of Syracuse and Aquila, brothers of the late king, had villas there, as had likewise many of the leading Neapolitan families... King Francis sent to the right-about, his uncles had to follow him into exile. Their villas at Sorrento were confiscated, and sold for what they would fetch – the Syracusa to some foreign lady of eccentric habits; the Aquila to Massa, the silk-mercer, of the Strada Toledo. One after another, the different families disposed of their villas to the hotel-keeping fraternity. The Villa Strongoli became the Hôtel Tramontana; the Villa Nardi, a dependence of the same; the Villa Santa-Severina, the Hôtel Gran Bretagne, and so on, through the entire list. Sorrento is now nothing more than a great caravansary, the only society to be had there that of the *table-d'hôte*. The fact of there being no Anglican chaplain, no mendicant friar of our Established Church duly licensed to preach the gospel of peace and make mischief, is sufficient proof that Sorrento is not a favorite resort of the English; for the "little flock" must be a very little flock indeed, that is so insignificant as to be considered not worth the trouble of "shepherding" by some needy emissary of the Continental... People who come to Sorrento hoping to find a little congenial society will be disappointed...

ALEXIS DE TOCQUEVILLE, *Memoir, Letters, and Remains* (1862)

Sorrento, January 5, 1851

... I find it hard to make acquaintances, though I am not particular as to the sort. The Italian middle classes, the only class to be found at Sorrento, do not care to visit you, because they do not care that you should visit them; and they do not care that you should visit them, because they live in garrets of which they are ashamed, and which they do not choose to convert into clean and comfortable apartments...

JULIA KAVANAGH, *A Summer and Winter in the Two Sicilies* (1858)

The social life of this little place is as un-English as its external aspect. Politics, libraries, books, clubs, concerts, ball-rooms, tea-gardens, public promenades, are absent. Dirty cafés, the streets, the piazza, and the churches, are the only places where the people meet on other errands than those of business. On Sunday evenings, I have seen men and women in holiday attire, with a sprinkling of priests and monks walking, and driving up and down the dusty road leading to Castellamare, so that I suppose there is a sort of pleasure in it. Now and then the sound of the tambourine issuing from some open doorway announced that girls were dancing in the court within; but this Sunday-dancing is thought neither pious nor respectable.

...

Such are the external features in the social life of Sorrento, which at once strike the most careless observer; but there is a great deal more which is not so soon apparent. The most important person in the place is the archbishop. He resides in rather a cheerless palace near the cathedral, and lives in a quiet, retired way. His large, antiquated carriage, drawn by sober black horses, sometimes appears in the Strada di Mezzo, which it almost fills; but he generally prefers walking on foot, attended by his secretary. He is a tall, white-headed man, of venerable aspect. He is respected, but rather feared as a rigorous disciplinarian. His predecessor was a mild old man, charitable to the poor, and universally beloved. We were in Sorrento when he died. I heard the death-bell toll, and inquired for whom? Our servant burst into tears, clasped her hands, and cried:

"Monsignore is dead! Our father is gone!"

Next to the bishop comes Baron .... He is of an ancient Sorrento family, and he is very rich. His wealth is scattered over the whole of the country under the shape of farms, orchards of oranges, and plantations of olive trees. He thus possesses that territorial importance which is far beyond the possession of mere money in a small place like this. He spends the winter in Naples, comes here in the month of June, and does not leave till November. He resides in a large and handsome house, with an arched gate ever open, and before which sits a lazy porter, who moves his chair according to the progress of the sun. Beyond the arch there is a vista of a garden, which is half orchard, half garden, and commands magnificent views of the sea. The mansion is large, and plentifully adorned with family portraits and ancient furniture. The upper floor is let to foreigners. When I learned this, I could not help expressing my surprise that a gentleman of high birth, with a handsome fortune, should let furnished apartments; but my informant gave me a characteristic reply.

"Baron .... has a great many relatives in Naples; and, if he did not let those spare rooms, he would never be rid of visitors."... His wife, who is known for her charity and goodness, is an amiable woman. Their daughters are handsome, but painfully shy. I once succeeded in drawing one so far out, that she went and fetched me her cat to look at; but it was a solitary triumph which I did not enjoy twice – cat and mistress relapsed into their primitive coldness.

Countess .... is another specimen of Sorrento aristocracy. She is of an ancient historical family, well known in the province, but misfortunes have reduced her sadly. She wears cotton dresses, and literally lives by letting apartments. The world is the world everywhere. Speak of her to her townsmen, and they will smile and say, "Ah, she is of an old family – very old; but, poor thing, she is so *poor!*"

It is said in pity, but in that pity which is akin to contempt. The countess, however, holds a high head, and will not be made free with. An English lady, captivated by her title, and who told me "what a dear old lady Countess .... was," took a liberty she never would have taken with an English countess of half the Italian lady's pedigree – she called upon her unsolicited. Countess .... was too polite and too politic to be rude to a possible lodger; but she was too haughty in her heart to be at the command of any foreign lady. She received Mrs. S......... very politely, and, as they were neighbours, watched her going out the next day, when, opening her window, she summoned to her one of the Italian residents of the villa where Mrs. S......... then was, and she thus addressed him:

"Don Sabino, do me the favour to tell the Signora Inglese that I called whilst she was out, and that I left my card." And with an amiable *buon giorno* she threw him a card, which he delivered with the message to the deluded English lady.

I admired three things in this: Italian pride of birth, which no ill-fortune can lower; Italian complicity in cheating the foreigner; and Italian carelessness in not crossing the street to deliver the card – the window was found the readier way, and the window was adopted.

...

The priests come between the aristocracy and the middle class. They are rather too numerous for the weal of the church; she is poor, and has neither revenues nor occupation for half of them, and half of them live on their private means. By many, especially in the middle class, the priesthood seems to be considered chiefly as an honour; young men become priests, in short, for their own pleasure and the gratification of their families, not because God called them to His altar, but because they must be gentlemen, and give distinction to an obscure race. This is a bad system, and the present Archbishop has partly earned his name of "rigoroso" by the efforts he makes to check it. He has turned out a good many young men from the seminary where he did not think they were wanted, wisely observing:

"A good layman is better than a bad priest."

... There are six convents in Sorrento, the monastery of San Paolo, where only ladies of noble birth are received; this is one of the few feudal relics of the place; another monastery, the convent Della Grazie, which is open to every class, and a conservatorio, or asylum, for poor girls, which has been founded by a charitable Canon, called the Santo. They are his children, and he gives them all he has. They are lodged free of expense, but must work for their support. They never go out, unless in case of illness. The Capucini have a convent some way out of Sorrento; they live on alms; the Franciscans, likewise a begging order, have a church and house in Sorrento; and the Jesuits have an old establishment and a fine garden near the sea. These six convents, two of which are supported by charity, are, nevertheless, the poor laws and the workhouses of Sorrento; every day the poor are fed and relieved at their gates...

The convents are the chief resources of the poor, yet it is but just to mention the assistance they derive from the various brotherhoods and corporations.

These associations are still found in French provinces and villages; but they are mere relics of the past; from England they have vanished entirely, since the Reformation; they still exist all over Italy. The subject is too interesting to be thus lightly dismissed. I shall speak of these brotherhoods, not merely as they exist in Sorrento, but as they are throughout the land. Their real spirit is not sufficiently known or understood.

The spiritual good of the members, and the spiritual and temporal good of that wide class which is known under the name of our neighbour, is the object of a religious brotherhood. Thus, when a man enters one of these associations, he voluntarily binds himself to certain devotions and penances; but chiefly to certain alms and charities.

The first time I knew what a religious brotherhood really is, was in Florence. We were looking at the Duomo, when a strange procession passed us. A sort of litter, carefully covered, was borne by men clad in dark-coloured robes, and whose faces were hidden by hoods. What were they carrying? Were they monks? What was it? We put these questions to a re-spectable-looking man, who smiled at our ignorance.

"They are carrying some sick or wounded person to the hospital," he replied; "they are not monks, but laies; Brothers of the Misericordia; the Grand Duke is the first, any honourable man, of any degree, may come af-ter him."

We looked at the feet of the brothers, the only index of their rank visi-ble, and we saw fine polished boots and coarse shoes.

"And does the Grand Duke really perform the duties of the brother-hood?" we asked.

"Certainly he does; he is called out in his turn."

AUGUSTUS J. C. HARE, *Cities of Southern Italy and Sicily* (1891)

... The peasants marry amongst one another – and, it must be allowed, to please their parents, for a house, a position – for anything but love...

JULIA KAVANAGH, *A Summer and Winter in the Two Sicilies* (1858)

The women are pretty much in the same position with the men. When they are ladies their life is retired, domestic, and dull. They marry, they en-ter a convent, or they become house-nuns; that is to say, they take the vows, but live at home like the virgins of the early church. But married women or nuns it seems that they must be...

It is rather a pitiable case that single women should be considered and should consider themselves as only fit to be locked up for life; but setting aside the immorality of doing from worldly reasons what should never be done save from the highest and purest motives, it should not be forgotten by those who condemn this system that these Italian nuns are at least pro-vided for. The poor girls who hunt for husbands for the sake of a position until great writers proclaim to the world in bitter and eloquent pages their misery and their degradation; the wide and unhappy class of gently ma-tured and educated women, who are flattered in the bloom of their youth, sneered at in its decline, made the butt of jests, more or less good natured, in their old age, who are handed about all their lives, the bore and burden of a family, who will teach your children for the sake of a home, who daily fill the columns of newspapers with their sad advertisements, and who are a living reproach to the society that gives them liberty and denies them its privileges, are here, either of them, unknown as a class.

Donna Anunziata, a pretty Sorrento girl, of eighteen, has given me on the important subject of marriages here, such precise information, that I shall give it in her own words, as the best illustration of Italian manners and habits, which differ so essentially from ours.

Donna Anunziata, as I said, is eighteen; she is short, and plump as a partridge; she has black hair, blue eyes, a Greek profile, white teeth, and rosy cheeks. She is one of the prettiest girls in Sorrento, and has already had one or two broken matches since we have been here...

"How is marriage conducted here?" I asked, in the course of our conversation.

Donna Anunziata opened her blue eyes at my ignorance, but replied in language more blunt than elegant; for, though well-born, she is ignorant, and she is naturally brusque.

"The mother of the young man goes to the mother of the young girl and says, 'I want this girl for my son.' The mother of the girl talks to her husband, the parents settle the money matters, and if the young people agree to it, it is a match."

This was rather brief; a little while afterwards she added, of her own accord: –

"I had a great deal more hair than that formerly; they say in Sorrento that when a girl is disappointed in marriage, she loses her hair; but I do not think so."

I agreed with her scepticism, and with a sigh Donna Anunziata soon added, giving a look at the mountains of Santa Agata, visible from our windows: –

"I was to have married up there, but I did not like the place."

"And that is a very important consideration in marriage," I suggested.

"The very first," she replied, solemnly.

The house was the first thing to think of; the husband came afterwards. I was amused at this lodger-like view of matrimony, but I remarked that if she had liked her bethrothed, she would have bourne even with Santa Agata. This was too romantic a flight for Italian matter-of-fact Donna Anunziata. She still stuck to her original opinion.

"Choose your house well."

"Then you did not like your betrothed?" I could not help saying.

"Yes, I did," she replied, a little testily; "but the Lord did not will it; it was not good for me, and in those things one must think of the soul," the beautiful blue eyes were turned up piously, "before the body."

"Poor lover," I thought; "the house and the soul, comfort and religion have combined against you."

"He was a fine young man," resumed Donna Anunziata, with a little sigh; "tall!" her eyes emphatically sought the ceiling; "shoulders like that;" she opened her arms wide. "And such health! A wrist that size," she added, uniting the fore-fingers and thumbs of her two hands. "And so good," she continued, "as good as a piece of bread... He was so good, in short, that he never spoke. Not even a word did he say. He would sit and say nothing. They say he is bigger and handsomer than ever; but what do I care?"

But she could not drop the subject; the lost lover's size, bigness, beauty, silence, and goodness had evidently impressed Donna Anunziata. She told me his name, Pietro, and his age, nineteen. He was very fond of her, and, spite his silence, had wasted away a good deal, perhaps through that sudden but fugitive wish of entering the cloister which Anunziata had manifested a few months back, on the death of her brother. Pietro, moreover, was always teazing his mother to bring Anunziata up to him at Santa Agata; and as the young lady always prudently declined the invitation, Pietro wept. Oh, yes! he was fond of her; no wonder; it had been going on a year; and their room was prepared in his mother's house. That mother, by the way, is a sort of ogress; she goes out with a stick and hunts in her sons before the Ave Maria, for parental authority is still strong and vigorous here. The marriage was agreed on, when the young girl's father thought it right to ask for a settlement, upon which they took the papers to examine them, went up to Santa Agata, and, as Anunziata naïvely expressed it, "they came down no more."

In short, it was a broken match.

Another lover soon made his appearance, "but he too," says Donna Anunziata, "went away, and did not come back."

"Did you like him?" I asked.

"Oh! yes," she replied; but I heard nothing about his beauty.

A little while afterwards she added pensively: –

"They say in Sorrento that a girl never forgets first love."

"They say that in other places, too," I remarked.

"Yes, but they say it in Sorrento," she persisted, "and it is true."

"Why do you not marry in Sorrento itself?" I asked; the second lover was from Massa; "are there no young men here?"

"There are three;" replied Donna Anunziata, with great quickness; "plenty of girls, but no men; only those *three.*"

The Community Celebrates

The community celebrations of harvest and of holy days is a frequent theme of foreign visitors' writings. These occasions "call together for one purpose all the classes" of the Sorrentine social world; they are joyous and devotional at the same time. The passages follow the ecclesiastical calendar, describing the Good Friday procession, Corpus Christi (June), the feast of the Immaculate Conception (December), and Christmas.

ARTHUR H. NORWAY, *Naples, Past and Present* (1901)

As the dusk descends upon Sorrento, and the sea turns grey, the narrow, tortuous streets resume an appearance of vast age. They are very silent at this hour; the shops are mostly closed; the children hawking woodwork have gone home. One's footsteps echo all down the winding alleys, and the tall houses look mysterious and gloomy. Such was the aspect of the town on the evening of Good Friday, when I took my stand in the garden of the Hotel Tramontano to see the procession of our Lady of Sorrows, who, having gone out at daybreak to seek the body of the Lord, has now found it, and is bearing it in solemn mourning through the city streets.

Along the narrow lane which passes the hotel a row of lamps has been set, and little knots of people are moving up and down, laughing and jesting, with little outward recognition of the nature of the rite. The procession has already started; it is in a church at the further end of the long alley, and every ear is strained to catch the first sound of the chanting which will herald its approach. Wherever the houses fall back a little the space is banked up with curious spectators. Some devout inhabitant hangs out a string of coloured lamps, and is rewarded by a shower of applause and laughter, which has scarcely died away when a distant strain of mournful music casts a hush over the throng. Far down the alley one sees the glittering of torches, and a slow, sobbing march, indescribably weird and majestic, resounds through the blue night, with soft beat of drum and now and then a clash of cymbals. Very slow is the approach of the mourners, but now there is no movement in the crowd. Men and children stand like ranks of statues, watching the slow coming of the torches and the dark waving banners which are borne behind them.

So the heavy rhythm of the funeral march goes up into the still air, knocking at every heart; and after the players, treading slow and sadly, come the young men of Sorrento, two and two, at wide intervals, hooded in deep black, their eyes gleaming through holes in the crape masks which conceal their faces. Each bears some one among the instruments of the divine passion – the nails, the scourge, and scourging pillar, the pincers – while in their midst rise the heavy folds of a huge crape banner, drooping mournfully from its staff. Next comes a silver crucifix raised high above the throng, and then, as the head of the procession winds away among the houses, the throbbing note of the march changes to a sweeter and more plaintive melody, while from the other hand there rises the sound of voices chanting "Domine, exaudi." In a double choir come the clergy of the city and the country round, all robed in solemn vestments, and between the two bodies the naked figure of our Lord is borne recumbent on a bier, limbs drawn in agony, head falling on one side, pitiful and terrible, while last of all Our Lady of Sorrows closes the long line of mourners.

When she has passed, silence drops once more upon the dusky alleys. Far off, the sound of chanting rings faintly across the houses, and the slow music of the march sighs through the air. Then even that dies away, and on the spot where Tasso opened his eyes upon a troubled world, there is no sound but the wind stirring among the orange blossoms, or the perpetual soft washing of the sea about the base of the black cliffs.

JULIA KAVANAGH, *A Summer and Winter in the Two Sicilies* (1858)

The real, the popular, and general source of amusement here is the Festa. It has two distinct aspects – the devotional and the joyous – and both are thoroughly southern. The expenses of the festa are voluntarily borne by rich and poor, according to their means; and the gaiety of church decoration, procession, music, and firing, is in exact proportion to the amount collected.

The church where the festa is kept is decorated, sometimes a week beforehand, with draperies of the cheapest materials, but bright in hue, and glittering with gilt paper, the whole pinned together with a dexterity, a grace, and a taste for contrast of colour, that are truly marvellous. The effect of these draperies, hanging in festoons between the arches, is extremely pretty, especially when all the waxlights are burning. But the painted cornices, false columns with Corinthian capitals, statues of wood, painted flesh colour and dressed in real garments, cannot be defended on any of the rules of taste or beauty...

Ringing of bells and firing of shots, throngs of people in holiday gear, going to and coming from the church, open the festa. The steps of the church are crowded; a popular preacher is expected, or the archbishop is to officiate. The vendors of fruit and gingerbread are at their stalls, screaming and selling; children have spent half the night in decorating the neighbouring doorways with draperies and in adorning little altars with flowers; a plate, covered with coppers, makes a silent but significant appeal to your generosity.

There are not many costumes about Sorrento, yet it is a living, moving sight. The red Phrygian caps of the men, the snow-white cambric or linen veils of the peasant-girls, the black lace veils of the middle-class ladies, the French bonnets of the little aristocracy, give vivacity to the crowd. Sometimes the wives of mountaineers come down from their haunts, and display costumes which have grown too antique here. A red-silk Phrygian cap, fastened above the forehead and falling behind, a close-fitting silk or cloth jacket, with gold-lace on every seam, and a long, ample, silk skirt, plaited from the waist to the feet in such close narrow folds that it looks more like a sack than a skirt, is one of the most characteristic costumes I have seen. A bright yellow apron and a quantity of chains, rings, and gold ornaments generally set it off.

But in the meanwhile the church fills. High mass is being sung within; the deep voices of monks, or the more tender tones of invisible nuns, blend with the pealing of the organ. A signal is given – it is the moment of the elevation – a deafening noise of petards follows. In this most unwarlike country, nothing can be done without powder.

So much for the morning of the festa; but if it be of the more solemn kind, the organ is silent. A regular orchestra has been erected in the church for musicians who came the evening before from Naples, armed with every possible instrument.

They come and go free of expense, and that is all the reward they get or expect for their trouble. The church or the convent gives them a lodging, the parishioners send beds and other necessaries, and thus the music is had, and little money is spent. The music in itself is generally excellent, though not always sacred. People here think like Wesley, that the devil shall not have all the good tunes; but they might, in all conscience, leave him a little more of his property, and observe more rigidly the decrees of the Council of Trent, to which the Catholic Church owes that pathetic and magnificient music which seems made to charm all ages and all nations.

...

Nothing of the kind, I am sorry to say, is ever heard here. If Palestrina could rise from his tomb in Saint Peter's, he would be shocked to think that, even after three hundred years, so little progress has been made in the art to which his lifetime was devoted. However, the Sorrentini are not particular – let the music be of the bright kind, and the musicians but keep time, they are content.

In the afternoon comes the procession. That of Corpus Christi, in June, was the most solemn. A long file of brotherhoods in their gowns, of monks in their habits, of priests in white surplices or gorgeous vestments, all bearing tapers, and preceded by their banners, poured out of the church into the narrow streets, singing as they went. Last came the archbishop, bearing the blessed sacrament under a canopy. Choir boys preceded him. They carried baskets filled with the shining petals of the yellow broom and tender rose leaves, which they scattered around them with a lavish hand. The windows were hung with red, blue, and yellow draperies; the walls of the orange-gardens and vineyards were thronged with girls, who showered down flowers until the pavement was bright as a carpet. Canopied altars had been erected at every spot where the procession was to rest; and every time it rested the bishop gave benediction to a kneeling crowd, whilst boys fired the petards that announced, miles beyond the mountains and across the sea, that Sorrento was rejoicing.

The procession is sometimes followed by illuminations and fireworks. Soon as dusk closes in, the streets are lit up with many-coloured lamps, varied by such devices as zeal and little means suggest. Two Chinese pagodas adorned the door of a barber's shop on the evening of the last festa, whilst above the gate of a more ambitious rival, a glass lantern turned round, displaying to the admiring crowd below a little black horse, car, and rider, for ever prancing in the air. After the illuminations come the fireworks, bright but brief. When they are over, the festa is thoroughly ended, the streets empty – every one goes home – and if ten strike at the cathedral, it is thought late. A little extra drinking sometimes takes place amongst the least sober portion of the community, but quarrelling and fighting there is none.

This is a festa; and a festa is the only token of public life which a place like this exhibits to a stranger's eye. It is the only occasion that calls together for one purpose all the classes of its little social world. Take away the festa, and what remains to the people? To work hard, live on little, and sink wearied and worn into a forgotten grave! – their lot, all the world over. In England they drink, and beat their wives; in France, they drink rather less, but they dance more; and whilst they dance the police must look on. Here they pray and make merry; and thrice happy in this, they do not separate joy from worship.

HERBERT M. VAUGHAN, *The Naples Riviera* (1925)

With the ripening of the oranges on the trees appear those strange creatures from the wilds of the Basilicata or Calabria, the *Zampognari*, who visit Naples and the surrounding district in considerable numbers. They usually arrive about the date of the great popular festival of the Immaculate Conception (December 8th) and remain until the end of the month, when they return to their homes with well-filled purses. In outward aspect these strangers resemble the stage-brigands that appear in such old-fashioned operas as *Fra Diavolo,* for they wear steeple-crowned hats with coloured ribands depending, shaggy goat-skin trousers, crimson velvet waistcoats, blue cloaks, sandalled feet and gartered legs. Their pale faces are unshorn, and their hair hangs in great tawny masses over neck and ears, which are invariably adorned with golden rings. These fellows come in pairs, one only, properly speaking, being the *zampognaro,* for it is he who carries the *zampogna* or classical bag-pipe of Southern Italy, whilst his companion is the *cennamellaro,* so called from his ear-splitting instrument, the *cennamella,* a species of primitive flute. The *zampogna* may be described as first cousin to the historic bag-pipes of Caledonia, for the sounds emitted strongly resemble the traditional "skirling" of the pipes; but no Scotchman even could pretend to delight in the shrill notes of the *cennamella.* The former at least of these two popular instruments of southern Italy was well known to the omniscient author of the Shakespearean plays, for in *Othello* we have a direct allusion to the uncouth braying music still made to-day by these outlandish musicians.

"Why, masters, have your instruments been in Naples, that they speak i' the nose thus?... Are these, I pray you, wind instruments?... Then put up your pipes in your bag, for I'll away: go; vanish into air; away!"

In the midst of their instrumental duet the two shaggy mountaineers are apt to break into a harsh nasal hymn in honour of the Virgin, to visit whose shrines at this season of the orange harvest is the main object of their Christmas migration to the Neapolitan shores. Very tastefully decorated are many of the Madonna's little sanctuaries in or near the orange groves, when the arrival of the *zampognari* is considered imminent. The tiny lamps are well trimmed and shine brightly, whilst heavy garlands composed of masses of bay or laurel or ilex leaves, interspersed with some of the golden clusters of the ripening fruit are suspended round the alcove that holds the figure of the Virgin. This effective but simple form of ornamentation will at once suggest the beautiful glazed and coloured terra-cotta wreaths of fruit and foliage that are to be seen so frequently in Tuscan churches; indeed, it is possible that the members of the Della Robbia family may have originally borrowed the decorative schemes for their famous plaques and lunettes from the rustic shrines thus simply but tastefully embellished. Nominally, the two performers are supposed to sing and make music on nine different days at the houses of all their patrons in order to make up the total number of the *novena,* but the extent of their performances is generally calculated in accordance with the depth of the householder's purse, the sum given for their services varying from a few *soldi* to a five *lire* note. All classes of society employ the *zampognari*, for it is with the first appearance of the lovely golden fruit, essentially *the* winter fruit of the Italians, that the arrival of these picturesque strangers has been associated from time immemorial. The *zampognari* are in fact as much of a national institution with the Neapolitans at Christmastide as are the waits or carol-singers in our own country, so that to the majority of these people *Natale senza zampogna e cennamella* would seem no true Christmas at all.

Closely connected with the life of the people of the Piano di Sorrento is the famous dance known as the *Tarantella*, which may be witnessed by the curious at almost any time – for money. Even when performed by professional dancers, tricked out in spick and span stage-peasant finery, the Tarantella is a most graceful exhibition of movement, although the dance naturally gains in interest when it takes place in the days of vintage or on the popular festivals of the Church, without the presence of largesse-giving strangers. The origin of the name has always puzzled antiquarians, although in all probability the dance derives its curious appellation from the Greek city of Taranto, whence the Tarentines introduced its steps and action into other parts of Italy. But vulgar belief is very strong, so that this graceful dance is still closely associated in the popular mind with the *tarantula*, a kind of poisonous spider found in the neighbourhood of Taranto, the effects of whose bite are said to yield to violent exercise followed by profuse perspiration. In order to excite the proper amount of exertion necessary for the cure, the person afflicted, *il tarantolato* is induced to leap and caper by the sound of music, with the result that there exist a number of tunes specially connected with this wild species of dancing. The real explanation of this fable seems to lie in the extremely excitable nature of the Tarentines themselves, assisted by the exhilarating music and by frequent pulls at the wine barrel. The two lines sung to the air of one of the tunes employed:

> "Non fu Taranta, ne fu Tarantella,
> Ma fu la vino della carratella:"
> ["It was neither the taranta, nor the tarantella,
> but it was the wine from the cask."]

sums up pretty accurately the real cause of these strange Tarentine orgies, which have really nothing whatever in common with the rhythmical dance that is still so popular in the environs of Naples. Nevertheless the theory of *tarantella* and *tarantismo* has been gravely discussed by old Italian writers, and a certain learned prelate of the fifteenth century, Niccolo Perotto, Archbishop of Siponto, alludes to the malignant cause of this dance-cure as "a species of speckled spider, dwelling in rents of the ground caused by excessive heat. It was not known in the time of our fore-fathers, but now it is very common in Apulia... and is generally called *Tarantula*. Its bite seldom kills a man, yet it makes him half stupid, and affects him in a variety of ways. Some, when a song or tune is heard, are so excited that they dance, full of joy and always laughing, and do not stop till they are entirely exhausted; others spend a miserable life in tears, as if bewailing the loss of friends. Some die laughing, and others in tears."

Such is the curious legend concerning the origin of the Tarantella, which is still danced with something of the old spirit by the holiday-making crowds of Naples, though it is at the *festa* of San Michele, the patron of Procida, that the Tarantella can now be seen to best advantage. Of the three islands that lie close to Naples, Procida is the least known or visited by strangers, so that when the Tarantella is danced by the Procidani, the old-fashioned popular orchestra is employed to give the necessary music. This consists of five quaint instruments (obviously of Oriental origin as their counterparts can still be seen amongst the Kabyles of Northern Africa): the first being a fife (*siscariello*); the second a tin globe covered with skin pierced by a piece of cane (*puti-puti*); the third a wooden saw and a split stick, making a primitive bow and fiddle (*scetavaiasse*); the fourth an arrangement of three wooden mallets, that are rattled together like a gigantic pair of bones (*tricca-ballache*); and the fifth a Jew's harp (*scaccia-pensieri*). A tarantella danced to the accompaniment of so weird a medley of instruments and by real peasants full of gaiety is naturally a thing altogether diverse from the stilted, though graceful and decorous performance that can be observed any day for payment in a Sorrentine or Neapolitan hotel; yet it must ever be borne in mind that the Tarantella proper, whether danced *con amore* by Procidan peasants or performed for lucre by costumed professionals, is no vulgar frenzied *can-can*, but musical love-dance expressive of primitive courtship.

W. J. A. STAMER, *Dolce Napoli* (1878)

The Tarantella is a choregraphic love-story, the two dancers representing an enamoured swain and his mistress. It is the old theme – "the quarrel of lovers is the renewal of love." Enraptured gaze, coy side-look, gallant advance, timid retrocession, impassioned declaration, supercilious rejection, piteous supplication, softening hesitation; worldly goods oblation, gracious acceptation; frantic jubilation, maidenly resignation. Petting, wooing, billing, cooing. Jealous accusation, sharp recrimination, manly expostulation, shrewish aggravation; angry threat, summary dismissal. Fuming on one side, pouting on the other. Reaction, approximation, exclamation, exoneration, reconciliation, osculation, winding up with a grand *pas di circomstane*, expressive of confidence re-established and joy unbounded. That's about the figure of it; but no word-painting can give an idea of the spirit, the "go" of the tarantella when danced for love and not for money.

JULIA KAVANAGH, *A Summer and Winter in the Two Sicilies* (1858)

... And Christmas here, though its joy does not take the aspect of coal fires, plum pudding, and roast beef, is merry Christmas for all that.

Three years ago, we were in Rome. We heard the Pope saying mass in Saint Peter's, and witnessed all the magnificence with which the Church commemorates the birth of Christ... But, for all that, I think that a Christmas in Sorrento will bear comparison with any Christmas, even with a Roman one.

It is ushered in with an awful slaughter of pigs, with festive preparations of every kind, and with an interchange of convivial presents. For some days before and after Christmas, but especially before, you cannot enter the streets or lanes of Sorrento without meeting men and boys gravely bearing on their heads the large, flat, tray-like baskets they here call "sporte," with a dainty white cloth thrown over them to conceal their contents from the curious. Three of these sporte have found their way to us.

The first that came contained a large quantity of those little red-cheeked apples, which the Italians hold for a rare and dainty fruit. I have noticed the sparkle of their eye when you ask them if it is good. Good! It is delicious. We were but half deceived; yet we gave these said apples a fair trial, and raw, boiled, or roasted, we found them shamefully deficient, unworthy of a place on the poorest London stall. The fact is, an Italian does not know what an apple is. However, this first sporta held something besides the little deceivers. It held large and magnificent oranges, with their stems and shining leaves; lemons, long, yellow, full of juice, and which the natives call bread lemons, and eat in slices, and little tender green lemons – oh! luxury unknown out of the land where the lemon grows – just plucked in their sweet unripeness from the tree. The peculiar flavour of these little green lemons must be left to imagination; it cannot be described.

The second sporta, or rather canestra, for it was an humble offering on a small scale, was part of a present which the contadina, who gave it to us, had received from the mountains of Arola. She sent oranges and lemons in summer, and got her winter return. It held the red-cheeked apples, of course, cones of the large, flat Italian pines that give a peculiar character to the Italian landscape, and which, (the cones, of course), are publicly sold and roasted in the streets of Naples; sorbinelle and chestnuts innumerable. Some were raw, more were baked and strung together in the shape of a lozenge. These baked chestnuts are as hard, or almost, as marble; but they are not without a certain pleasing taste, which the owners of good teeth can appreciate.

The third sporta was in higher style, and altogether an ambitious affair. Its contents, when emptied out, covered a whole table. Apples, of course, dried figs, dried cherries, green lemons, pears, (as good as the apples, if not better), nuts, without end, made a splendid show.

A blue paper, when opened, showed some excellent sweets, made by the fair hands of the noble ladies of the monastery of Saint Paul, who, like all nuns, have distinguished talents in that line; then came a large delicious melon from Rocca di Papa, and finally a plate with the national cotone.

The day before Christmas is a fast-day, and, unless a Neapolitan observes the fast by having a cotone for his supper, he is not happy.

The cotone is to him, what roast beef and plum pudding are to a thorough-bred Englishman on Christmas day. What is Christmas eve without that dish? It is not Christmas at all. Accordingly, a real Neapolitan – the Sorrentini have a hankering after the cotone, but do not go into excesses – a real Neapolitan will, I have been assured, over and over, sell his bed and sleep on the floor rather than not sup on this cotone. And what do you think this cotone is? Why, it is an eel, twisted in a circle, with laurel-leaves around it, and three green lemons within. It is to be cut in small pieces; each piece is put between two laurel-leaves; the whole is fried in oil, served up hot, and eaten with the juice of the green lemons squeezed over it, and a very savoury dish it is.

The religious ceremonies begin on Christmas eve, and are continued the whole night long. One of them is peculiar to Sorrento. I had often heard of it from the Sorrentini, and greatly wished to see it.

At six we went to the church of the Congregazionella. It is kept by the Servi di Maria, who are all nobles; vain relic of feudal times and of a lost power. A very dashing young aristocrat, Dom Francesco, no sooner understood that we were foreigners, than he handed us to the best front seats – one constantly receives these marks of hospitable courtesy from the Italians. The church is a pretty church, and it was gaily decorated and brilliantly lit. To the left of the crimson altar stood a gilt and red velvet chair. It was waiting for the Bambino Gesu. The child Jesus was to sit on that chair, and be honoured that night.

An ancient custom, of which the origin is forgotten, but which is still religiously observed in Sorrento, decrees that on the night of the birth of Christ, a real child, living and beautiful, shall be chosen as the representative of the divine child our eyes are not blessed in beholding, and that the faithful, like, the shepherds of Bethlem, like the Eastern Kings, shall come and offer him gifts, and pay him homage.

We had not been seated long, when two side-doors opened – on one side, priests came out, on the other, a brown, good-looking woman, bearing a young child of three or so in her arms. He was a beautiful dark-eyed boy, clad royally in a cloak of scarlet wool. His mother placed him sitting on the red-velvet chair, and, removing the cloak, showed him in his little white shirt, bare-footed and bare-armed. A gilt basin and ewer, and a sponge, were handed to one of the priests. He took them, and, kneeling before the child, he washed the feet of this little heavenly ambassador. He next shod him with stockings and embroidered shoes. After this, the child was placed standing, a little silk frock of blue, with pink bows, made by his mother, and not in the least emulating the Hebrew costume, was thrown over him. Finally, the priest placed on his head a crown of flowers. Each act was accompanied by prayers in Italian. No sooner was the child crowned, than shots were fired without, and the Servi di Maria, all rising, opened the Te Deum. The boy remained standing the whole time it was sung. His father supported him, and helped him to hold his little right arm, on which a bag of sweets had been hung, in the act of benediction, which the old painters give to the child Jesus. He behaved with great decorum, and only once showed some emotion. When the shoes were placed on his feet, he smiled, and turned his head of one side, looking at them with evident delight.

When the Te Deum was over, his mother took him in her arms, and carried him away. As she passed by us, her brown face beamed with happiness. Indeed, I never saw so much smiling in a church before. The priests, the Servi di Maria, the boys and men, who, with Italian familiarity, crowded around the altar, the ladies in the front seats, the contadine behind, were all one flow of smiles as they looked at the Bambino.

After his departure, the religious ceremonies proceeded. We had a sermon from a Canon, an address from the Archbishop, and Benediction. I heard, on the following day, more details concerning this pretty ceremony.

Formerly, the poorest child was chosen, and this was fit. A nun embroidered his habit, and kept him at her cost for a year; but now the nun is dead. The poor cannot bear the expense of the child's attire, and the rich and the comfortable have stepped in and taken possession of the post for their own children. The candidates must present themselves a year before the appointed time. Beauty is the greatest recommendation; next to beauty comes poverty. The poorest among the comfortable have the best chance. This year's Bambino Gesu is our neighbour. He is the son of a blacksmith, a little way off down the lanes; and his father has informed our servant Maria that it is a great consolation to him to have the divine child in his home. When this young king, whose name is Salvatore, left the house to proceed to the church, shots were fired, shots were fired when he came back, shots were fired when he got up the next morning, shots were fired when he sat down to his Christmas dinner – in short, his happy father's pocket was fairly drained by gunpowder.

Well, it is a beautiful custom, worthy of a poetic people, whose thoughts must ever take a visible and poetic form. I felt, as I looked at that child, born to sorrow, sin, and death – I felt that it is good to be thus reminded of mysteries we treat so spiritually that we sometimes forget them. Do we, indeed, always remember that Christ became a weak little child for our sakes? We know it, but do we think much of it? Ay, truly I felt, as I looked on – as I saw the ardent faith of this simple people – ay, truly this is the flesh of Christ – this is the real humanity to which he became wedded, which he redeemed by his birth as well as by his blood.

The function over, we went to Gargiulo's, the falegname known to all the visitors of Sorrento for his elegant wood-work. He had very civilly asked if we should like to know from his household what takes place in most Sorrento families on Christmas eve, and as this was a thing we greatly desired, we accepted willingly. Accordingly his son and two workmen came and fetched us, not for protection, for Sorrento is a safe place, but to light our path with lanterns – no useless precaution; lamps and gas are unknown here, and, unless when the moon shines, the streets are so many pits of darkness.

We were introduced into a large room, where the presepio had been made on boards raised about two feet above the ground. It was a stylish one, a large one too, but, first of all, what is a presepio? It is a representation of the birth of Christ. It is made of wood, of stumps of trees, of moss, of anything that will answer, and it represents rocks, rivers, trees, castles, houses, villas, palaces, anything that comes into the head of the contriver; provided that, in the centre, there be a spot which may be called the stable of Bethlem, and which will accomodate the Holy Family. Little baked clay figures, painted in strong colours, of shepherds bringing gifts, of animals, of peasant men and women, of pilgrims, kings, lords, and ladies, of angels too, with wonderful wings, playing on fiddles, and hanging from wires, are indispensable for a presepio. It is to the Italian children what the Christmas tree is in Germany.

The little waxen image representing the holy child was not yet in the manger of Gargiulo's presepio. The youngest boy, Ferdinando, who was gaily dressed in blue, with a red scarf and white frill, and whose grave face never relaxed into a smile, went out for the purpose of carrying this image processionally in the streets, and bringing it to the presepio with due solemnity.

Vengono – vengono! cried his mother and sisters with great eagerness. They threw the windows open, and requested us to look out. We saw lights coming along the dark street, we heard deep male voices singing the Te Deum, and under a dais we saw the grave Ferdinando, solemnly carrying the Bambino.

The procession entered the house, the Bambino was brought in, laid in the manger by Ferdinando, and the whole band began singing little Christmas hymns; next appeared Gargiulo's eldest son, a lad of fourteen, with priest's cap, cassock, and surplice. He ascended a temporary pulpit gaily decorated with tinsel, and on the text, "parvulus natus est," he delivered a flourishing sermon; the emphasis and gestures were perfect, and the self-possession complete. When he had done, the hymns began again, and wine and cakes, the gifts of the shepherds, we were told, went round. The ease, the good-breeding of these men, the absence of vulgarity in their manners and appearance, struck me very forcibly. I was seated by a Neapolitan lady, who had come to spend an hour with Gargiulo's family and presepio.

"I felt dull alone," she said, "and Gargiulo is a civil sort of man," she added, condescendingly.

It seems she had heard we were coming, and was most anxious to make our acquaintance.

"Neapolitans are such animals," she whispered, with a frown of disgust, "and foreigners are *so* amiable."

I ventured to suggest that all Neapolitans might not be so very animal as she thought, nor yet all foreigners so very amiable; but she squeezed my arm, and with an expressive look, reiterated her assertion, "sono bestie," for her unfortunate countrymen, and "cosi gentili" for the whole foreign brood.

We had another amateur of Gargiulo's festivities in the person of a tall Sorrento cavalier, who was a great deal more civilized than the Neapolitan lady. But well-bred conversation is not graphic, and he said nothing worth repeating.

The solemnity of the presepio being over, we left. The whole family, however, religiously spent the evening in eating and drinking. To go to bed on Christmas Eve is held unlucky. Accordingly, there was nothing in the street but carrying Bambini about with tapers, and firing of petards, and singing of Te Deums, and nothing but eating sweets and drinking wine and liqueurs within doors. Fighting, quarrelling, drunkenness, are unknown in this happy country – it is all merry-making and devotion.

During Christmas time, the presepio of Dom Sabino is open to the public. We went to see it to-day. It fills a room; and the figures are ten inches high, at the very least.

Well, imagination is a fine thing, and Dom Sabino has got plenty of it. He is the author of all the fine presepii in and about Sorrento; and his terra-cotta figures have been purchased and carried away by enthusiastic foreigners, especially by Americans. They are, as I said, terra-cotta – the faces and hands are very carefully painted, and the clothes are not shabby, baked clay, but real clothes of silk and velvet; and this especially excites the admiration, as well it may, of all Sorrento.

But, indeed, this presepio is very pretty, and what is there not in it? Fair princesses, covered with pearls; wealthy peasant women, in national costume; one old lady, grim and brown, is riding on a horse; shepherds making cheeses; naked beggars, clad in patches, and screaming out their misery to his eccellenza, one of the kings riding by; a shepherd playing on his pipes, and rivalling the melody of the angel above; besides dogs, cats, rabbits, the ox, the ass, and the star – large and brilliant as a planet – are all there, every one of them.

The holy family is not very visible; but I thought that the fair face of the Madonna looked very sweet. Saint Joseph was venerable; and the kneeling king, who humbly worshipped the divine child, struck me with his royal look.

The details, the episodes of this little drama are not amongst its least interesting features. Dom Sabino is a poet and a philosopher. On the ruins of a Roman temple he has raised a poor, modern shop, filled with all sorts of eatables. He has a turn for the popular, too. A fiddler playing on a loggia, a group of itinerant musicians, are all excellent in their way. But, oh! ye Moorish slaves, bending beneath the weight of that velvet chest, with its silver clasps! – ye knights and pages of the crescent – was there a crescent then? – with your prancing horses housed in richest velvet! – ye pious kings and wise men of the East, who shall recount your glories? – who but that contadina on the rocks that overlooks the path! Her outspread hands and open mouth express her admiration, and, in their turn, excite that of a real, living contadina by me. With Italian familiarity, she laid her hand on my shoulder, and, pointing with the other hand to the little clay figure, she chuckled with admiration and glee.

Dom Sabino himself – a dignified-looking gentleman, though not enthusiastic – was not his own coldest admirer. He heard our praise modestly; but when we forgot the expression of that face, or the turn of this figure, he gently drew our attention, and let us miss nothing.

Sites and Insights for the Visitor

"Fruits of the earth"

Before tourism began to expand so lucratively in the eighteenth century, agriculture was of primary importance for the local economy. The cultivation of olive trees, vineyards and citrus groves continues today, although on a smaller scale. Intensifed competition in the twentieth century has seriously diminished the production and trade of oranges. A few fruit-laden trees can still be found on the streets and squares of Sorrento; one road is even named "Via degli Aranci." The sweet smell of orange blossoms and exquisite taste of the oranges and lemons of Sorrento are still celebrated today; their excellence is thought to be the result of the particularly mild climate of the region. The last decade has seen a boom in the production of an after-dinner lemon liquor called limoncello *which is served chilled in iced glasses. Perfumes, soaps and other items employing oranges and lemons are available in many shops for tourists.*

Sorrento's cornucopia of fresh produce is displayed every day in the abundant and colorful arrangements carefully prepared by the vendors along Via San Cesareo. To experience the pain and joy of animated haggling and bargaining, the visitor can attend one of the weekly markets in Sorrento and other towns on the peninsula (check tourist information offices for the locations and days of the week).

Sorrento is known for other local food products such as olive oil, cheese called treccia *(braided* fior di latte*), and walnuts. A special liquor (*nocillo*) is made from Sorrentine walnuts.*

Diners have their choice of many local dishes in Sorrento's wonderful and numerous restaurants. Besides the fresh seafood and traditional Neapolitan cuisine, Sorrento is known for gnocchi alla Sorrentina *(potato dumplings with tomato sauce and melted mozzarella cheese) and* cannelloni alla Sorrentina. *Tempting pastries are all too easily available, as are some of the best ice creams in Italy. In short, the food in Sorrento is an essential ingredient in the visitor's experience of earthly paradise.*

"Fruits of labor"

Sorrentine artisans continue to produce and sell their crafts in the historic center's narrow streets, although it has become more difficult to find authentically hand-crafted items. The once flourishing and highly esteemed local silk industry has gradually disappeared over the years. But silk goods – in the form of silk ties and scarves made elsewhere – are still for sale. So too are embroidered cloth, damask, and laces, some of them still hand-made locally. Wood inlay furniture and objects (intarsia) have been produced in Sorrento since the nineteenth century and are popular souvenirs. They range widely in quality and in design. Hand-painted ceramics in the tradition of Vietri sul Mare on the Amalfi coast and coral and cameos associated with the area near Torre del Greco are also available.

Religious traditions and holidays

According to tradition, Christianity was introduced into the Sorrento area by the apostle Saint Peter. Legend has it that he stopped at a place near today's border between Sorrento and Sant'Agnello on his way to Rome.

The patron saint and protector of Sorrento is Saint Antonino Abate; his feast day is celebrated on February 14. One of the miracles attributed to him is his rescue of a child swallowed by a big fish. A statue is dedicated to him in Piazza Tasso, as is a church in the square bearing his name.

The most impressive and moving of the numerous festivities in Sorrento are the processions during Holy Week. On Good Friday, the "white" confraternity's procession at three o'clock in the morning features a worried Madonna (represented by a statue) searching for her Son. The evening's mournful "black" procession, by a second confraternity, shows the sorrowful Madonna weeping behind the bier of Christ. People come from all over Italy and the world to attend these beautiful and haunting displays of the Passion. Crowds then enjoy the tradition of Pasquetta, *a picnic in the countryside on the Monday after Easter.*

Sorrento is also a picturesque place to spend Christmas; there are concerts, zampognari *(pipers), and local treats to try like roasted chestnuts and* torrone *(nougat candy). The celebratory family meal still features* seafood, although the traditional eel is gradually losing its prominence at the table. The Sorrentine variations of the presepi or crib scenes are also major attractions. The visitor can stop at each church in town and delight in the original ways that Sorrentine scenery, customs, and food are incorporated into the traditional manger scene. Of particular beauty is the presepio in the Duomo. A very large and complex presepio in the Sedile Dominova takes about a month to set up and also draws crowds of admirers.

CHAPTER 6

CAPTURED BY SIREN LAND

The average tourist in Italy sees very little that is distinctively Italian. The places he visits have been visited by such an infinite number of tourists before him that they have acquired a certain tourist color, so to say, and have suffered a certain localization of small iniquity which passes in the eyes of foreigners for native character... He and his colleagues in the land come to the most beautiful place in the world, stay three days in the modern hotel, drive a dozen miles or so over a modern road in a particularly shaky modern carriage, read "Agnes of Sorrento," and go to the next place mentioned in the guide-book.

F. MARION CRAWFORD

Regrettably, a modern tourist cannot easily duplicate the extended visit of a careful observer like Julia Kavanagh (see Chapter 5). Nowadays, reading about the Sorrento seen by others must serve as a substitute for those who stay in Sorrento only briefly. Still, reading about others' experiences has its own decided charms: this is tourism without stinging insects or noisy *motorini*!

Two of Sorrento's most fascinating commentators in the years after Kavanagh are F. Marion Crawford and Norman Douglas, for both of whom the area was home. Crawford's principal residence for much of his adult life was his coast villa in Sant'Agnello di Sorrento, and Douglas lived on the island of Capri from which he explored and wrote about the whole of Siren Land.

The two men shared a cosmopolitan upbringing and many gifts of the intellect and spirit. Douglas, a Scot, was actually born and spent his early years in Austria. The American Crawford was born in Rome (his father was a noted sculptor in the American expatriate community). Both men traveled widely in youth and throughout their lives, and neither set up a home base in the country of his citizenship. Crawford is reputed to have been fluent in eighteen languages – he kept his private notebook in Urdu. Douglas too was a polyglot; by the age of eighteen he had published scientific research papers in both English and German. Both men wrote keenly and observantly about the area they loved.

F. Marion Crawford

Although a college dropout (he left Cambridge after a year), Marion Crawford rarely met a profession, a craft, a trade, that he did not master. He was a skilled sailor and navigator; he held a captain's license, first class. With the help of a competent if illiterate Italian foreman, he designed and executed masterful architectural projects including the imposing seawall of his Villa Crawford, a monumental feature of the sea approach to Sorrento. He was a favorite tenor partner to the celebrated diva Nellie Melba (his lifelong friend) for drawing-room duets. He successfully directed a protracted lawsuit against the United States government on behalf of his father-in-law's company. And, because he could never have imagined settling down to a routine job, he mastered the craft of novel writing and supported his family through his pen for most of his life. It is said that he worked himself to death trying to provide for his wife and four children. Certainly he died young, and the record of his life reveals long periods of serious illness. All the more impressive, then, his remarkable achievements. Crawford's numerous friends all agree that to know him was to love him (the notable exception is Norman Douglas, whose essay on Crawford is found in the second half of this chapter).

When Marion Crawford died in Sorrento in April, 1909, Mayor Tramontano himself issued a funeral proclamation praising Crawford's love for his adopted home and the many volumes he'd written while resident there, volumes reflective of Sorrento's incomparable beauty and climate and the gentle souls of its inhabitants. A small part of one such volume, *To Leeward*, is printed below, preceded by a segment of Crawford's essay on the kind of "tourist" experience he seems to feel everyone should have.

"Coasting by Sorrento and Amalfi" reveals Crawford's Romantic sensitivity to place, and also that he could sometimes be biting in his judgments. The brief dips into Crawford's novel fairly illustrate the way he makes practical use of the landscape around him as backdrop to storylines only casually related to their setting. Crawford's novels may seem

View of Villa Crawford in Sant'Agnello

somewhat dated to today's reader. Still, they apparently put Sorrento on the map at least as far as the municipality was concerned. A street remains named after him.

F. Marion Crawford, "Coasting by Sorrento and Amalfi" (1894)

The *genius loci* of the ancients is not altogether a myth. A truer mysticism than their mythology teaches us that places retain for ages something of the lives that have been lived in them, an echo of the voices that have made them musical, a fleeting shadow of the men and women who found in them their happiness or their sorrow. Those who have spent much time in secluded spots learn to feel that lonely places have souls; and the soul of a place is indeed its *genius loci*, its familiar spirit, its peculiar essence, as real a thing as the scent of a rose or the smell of the sea. There are rose-gardens in the East that are fair with the accumulated happiness of past generations. There are shady ilex-groves in Italy wherein still dwells the silent spirit of contemplation; perhaps the phantasms of tragic loves sigh out their little day beneath the ancient trees. In Italy, in Greece, in Asia, in distant Indian glens, dim temples stand to this day, haunted or blest, perhaps, by the presence of that mystic spirit which outlasts all ages. And the market-place has its familiar genius also, the busy center of the crowded city, the broad thoroughfare of the great metropolis, silent for a few hours under the summer moonlight or the winter rain. Old castles too, deserted villages, uninhabited homes of dead populations – all have wraiths, the ghosts of what they have been, silent to the many, but more eloquent to the few than any human speech can ever be. And besides all these, there are spots where nature has never been molded by man, where she is sovereign and he is subject – lonely places by the sea, great sunlit silences where man has not dared to dwell because nature there would give him nothing, nor was he able to take anything from her. And the spirit of those places is more lonely, and grander, and mightier, than the *genius loci* of the market-place, or of the deserted Italian villa, "where the red dog-star cracks the speechless statues," or even of the shady cloister or of the wind-swept temples of banished gods. The song of songs is still unwritten, though nature's music makes man's grandest symphonies ridiculous, and sounds night and morning in the ears of him who has ears to hear.

But those are not the ears of the Cook's tourist, the German water-color painter, or the English spinster, all of whom come yearly southward to the Sorrento coast, as regular in their migration as the swallow, and far more welcome to the bankrupt hotel-keeper and the starving boatman, though less suggestive of poetic thoughts when a prominent object in the landscape. They come, they eat, they sleep, and their scarlet guide-books catch the sun and mark them for the native's prey. And then, thank heaven! they go. But it is easy to get away from them, for they keep to the beaten track, a vast flock of sheep for most of whose actions Mr. John Murray of Albemarle street will be held responsible at the last judgment. It may be doubted whether any church, any creed, or any despotic form of government which the world has ever seen, has disposed more completely of men's consciences, men's money, and men's movements, than the compilers and publishers of famous guide-books. Mr. Murray says to the tourist, "Go," and he goeth, or, "Do this," and he doeth it, in the certain consciousness that he cannot do wrong, which is more than the spiritual pastors and masters of the world generally succeed in accomplishing without assistance. I will not venture to impugn the judgment of the great guide-books, but I will venture to say that the average tourist in Italy sees very little that is distinctively Italian. The places he visits have been visited by such an infinite number of tourists before him that they have acquired a certain tourist color, so to say, and have suffered a certain localization of small iniquity which passes in the eyes of foreigners for native character. The least prejudiced of tourists is perhaps the German artist. He is also as a rule the most ready to undergo small hardships and considerable fatigue in the pursuit of the beautiful. But even he sees little. To him Capri seems wild, Naples picturesque, and Vesuvius romantic, and when he has painted the Capri Needles, has eaten shell-fish at Santa Lucia, and has picked up a handful of scoriae on the edge of the crater, he has generally had his fill of southern Italy, and goes home to talk about it. So far as Sorrento is concerned, he and his colleagues in the land come to the most beautiful place in the world, stay three days in the modern hotel, drive a dozen miles or so over a modern road in a particularly shaky modern carriage, read "Agnes of Sorrento," and go to the next place mentioned in the guide-book. It never seems to strike them that they could hire a little boat with a couple of men for a week, and wander in and out among the rocks and caves and beaches and fishing-villages all the way from Sorrento to Paestum, seeing sights not dreamed of in their guide-books, and calling up visions of the great romantic past, of Amalfi's doges, of Robert Guiscard, Tancred, and Pope Hildebrand, or else idle away half a day with the old fishermen of Crapolla or Prajano, listening to their strange tales, their stories of Arabian Nights in Italian dress, their amazing versions of Scripture history, and, more interesting still to those who love the sea, to their accounts of hairbreadth escapes in winter storms and summer squalls. And yet it is very easy to do all these things, and very pleasant, and there is no particular hardship to be undergone. Macaroni is not bad eating, and to most people it is a pleasant novelty to dine on mackerel, lobster, red mullet, or muraenae, just out of the sea. There is nothing particularly uncomfortable, either, in sleeping in the warm, dry sand, or in a boat-house on a pile of nets, or even in the bottom of the boat itself, with the Bay of Naples or the Gulf of Salerno for a bathtub in the morning, and the Southern moonlight for a bedroom candle.

Far be it from me to inflict upon any one who reads this sketch a history of Sorrento, or a dissertation upon the antiquities of the peninsula and the republic of Amalfi. The charm that clings to so many spots in Italy does not lie in the accurate knowledge of what has been, so much as in dreaming of what might have been, or may have been, or may yet be. The memory of one or two names, great, romantic, or even mythological, which live in the tales told by the people, has power to call up wonderful pictures. And sometimes wild places, rugged and lonely, to which no shadow of definite tradition belongs, appeal even more directly to the human heart.

Here the sirens still breathe the sea spray, and sing in the enchanted moonlight as Ulysses, lashed to the mast, sweeps by in his dark ship. Still, in the misty dawn, or in the purple twilight, the Barbary pirate's shadowy craft steals silently shoreward, laden with murder and fire and sudden death, but watched from a hundred towers, from which the warning beacon of smoke or flame will presently shoot up to the Southern sky. On those same sirens' isles, blind wretches still starve out their life on the remembrance of the greatness they misused for a little while over there in Amalfi, the price of which was blindness, hunger, and solitude. Here, under the Sorrento Cape, in the rock-girt bath of Joanna, the laughter of the queen and her court ladies still rings in tune with the ripple of the wind-blown water. Far back in the other gulf to southward, above Atrani, stands the solitary Devil's Tower wherein, in darker moods, Joanna performed her incantations; while farther still, away in Salerno, in Guiscard's city, her mother, Margaret of Anjou, sleeps beneath the marble canopy of her lovely tomb.

It is easy to fancy them alive again as one lies under the shadow of the rocks at noon-day, or by the water's edge when the moon is full, or as one steers in and out along the fantastic shore; the truth of history becomes a very secondary consideration, and the weird tales of the old man of Ellera seem very probable. The story-teller of the crew gives us an appalling version of Sinbad's adventure with the roc, as the embers of the camp-fire die away, and none of us would be much surprised if the gigantic bird loomed up suddenly behind the tower on the cliff, to descend bodily in the very midst of us with an Eastern prince or two in his beak. It is fairy-land, after all, and why should anything be too improbable to happen?

So much has been said of Sorrento itself, and so many people see it nowadays, that it seems hardly worth while to enter into a description of what many will allow to be the most beautiful spot in the world. As a rule, too, all description is a failure unless it appeals in some slight degree to memory. I might give a long account of its strange geological conformation; I might talk of its marvelous climate, for the Bay of Naples is the coolest place in Italy on the sea-level; I could describe its more or less civilized people, its oranges and lemons and olives, and even its extremely modern hotels: but he who sees and knows Italy dwells not in large buildings illuminated by electric light, and made lively by the perpetual whisk of the waiter's coat-tails, and though a man might spend many months in Sorrento, and gaze to satiety upon the lovely view, he might not see anything that would strike him as strange if he had much experience of the world, nor hear anything more amusing than the conversation of his fellow-tourists. We all know what that is like. Two of the species meet in their own country. "Where have you been?" "Egypt." "Ah, yes; Egypt. I remember Cairo. Capital steak at Shepheard's." But even in progressive Sorrento there are quiet villas far from electric lights and steak-critics, and underneath the villas at the base of the long perpendicular cliffs are green and blue caves, and natural arches, and deep openings to unfathomable Roman quarries. And there are gorges, too, in the hills, and lovely walks when one has got above the range of the narrow, high-walled lanes among which it is so hard to find one's way. There are endless fruit-trees, besides the orange and lemon, and there is everywhere and all summer an abundance of fruit – real Italian fruit, always unripe or over-ripe, but pretty to look at, and not poisonous. About Sorrento also there is something of a Neapolitan flavor in the air. The Neapolitan small boy is half monkey, half comedian, and all thief, and here as elsewhere the boy is father to the man. In Sorrento there is the municipal band, more inexorable in Italy than death itself; there are little companies of men and women who dance the tarantella in costume on the terraces of the hotels, and sing vulgar songs, which the foreigner takes for national airs. There are not, indeed, so many beggars as in Naples itself and its neighborhood, but the perpetual attempt to extract small coin from the visitor occupies the sole and undivided attention of at least one portion of the population. Here, as in Naples, the guide guides not, but chatters, butchering what he supposes to be the foreigner's language in order to make himself a holiday. Here, as elsewhere, the lively donkey boy twists the patient ass's tail, ultimately requests you to dismount at the steep places, and gets on himself. Here, as in all southern Italy, the small deceptions of a very poor and not very clever people bring a smile to the keen but often good-natured Northerner's face. All this I might describe at endless length had it not been done so often, and in one or two instances so well. There it all is, more or less lovely as to its surroundings, more or less modern in its buildings, more or less civilized by the people that move upon the scene. And below it, and before it, and facing it, stretches the sea, the eternal, ever-changing, ever-abiding sea. The splashes of human-wrought color, and the deeper tones of man-planted orange-gardens, and olive-groves, and vines, are forever contrasted with God's own palette, with that broad water wherein are mingled the precious things of day and night, the maiden rose-mallow of dawn, and the gorgeous purple of imperial evening, the gold of the sun and silver of the moon and the precious stones of the stars, all blending at last in the depths of the great liquid sapphire of that sea which wise men of old believed to be the source of all living things.

Here at least, if he chooses, man can leave dusty lanes and gorges, Neapolitan dances and improved hotels behind, and be alone with the sea a day, a week, or a month. There is no lack of boats, or of men who know the coast better than the lanes up there behind the town. There is no waiting for ebb or flow by this tideless water; by day or night, when fancy whispers the word, you may be borne swiftly and safely westward, by the rocks, round the Capo di Sorrento, past the Capo di Massa, in full sight of Capri, and altogether beyond civilization.

F. MARION CRAWFORD, *To Leeward* (1892)

[THE STORY SO FAR: *A pleasant Italian nobleman, Marcantonio Carantoni, and his English bride, Leonora Carnethy, are newly wed. They have settled in Sorrento for an extended honeymoon, in a villa very much like Marion Crawford's own. Leonora, young and a bit frivolous, had thought she would find marriage more ecstatic than it has proved to be with steady, affectionate Marcantonio. Into their lives comes Julius Batiscombe, a handsome, cosmopolitan man who shares several personal qualities with Crawford himself, including a successful career as a writer. Batiscombe is given to extended inner reflections, one of which reveals his sole weakness – he is, alas, a womanizer despite himself, and he feels awful about it. Not hard, then, to predict what happens after Batiscombe presents his card at Casa Carantoni, renewing an earlier social acquaintance with bored-to-tears Leonora. Batiscombe asks the Carantonis to accompany*

him in his yacht to watch a boat launching at Castellammare; we join the
story as he returns to his lodgings in the throes of anticipatory remorse.

Crawford himself mildly regretted having written To Leeward; *he*
judged it the only one of his novels that was not entirely proper. Its "im-
propriety" is not really noteworthy to a reader of today. What is there to
be enjoyed is a slice of aristocratic life not normally glimpsed by the visi-
tor, against Sorrento's scenic backdrop.]

... The fact was that Julius Batiscombe in love was one person, and
Julius Batiscombe out of love, repentant and trying to make up to the
world for the mischief he had done, was quite another; and he knew it himself. He was perfectly conscious of his own duality, and liked the one state,
– the state of no love, – and he loathed and detested the other both before
and after.

And now he sat over his coffee, and the prophetic warning of his soul
told him that he was in danger, so that he was angry at himself and feared
the future. He had known Miss Carnethy... for some time, and had danced
with her and sat beside her at dinner more than once, without giving her a
thought; he therefore had found it perfectly natural to call when he discovered that she was at Sorrento. But his impression after his visit was very different. The Marchesa Carantoni was not Miss Carnethy at all.

She had looked so magnificent as she sat in the evening sunshine, and
he had gazed contentedly at her with a sense of artistic satisfaction, thinking no evil. But now he could think of nothing else. The sun seemed to rise
again out of the dark sea, turning back on its course till it was just above
the horizon, with a warm golden light; by his side sat the figure of a woman
with glorious red hair, and he was speaking to her; the whole scene was
present to him as he sat there, and he knew very well what it was that he
felt. Why had he not known it at first? He would surely have had the sense
not to propose such a thing as a day together. "A day together" had so often entailed so much misery.

Nevertheless he would not invent an excuse, nor go away suddenly. It
would be quite possible, he knew, and perhaps also he knew in his heart
that it would be altogether right. But it seemed so uncourteous, he was really anxious to see the launch of the great ship and – and – he would not
be such a fool as to fancy he could not look at a woman without falling in
love with her on the spot. At his age! Five and thirty – he seemed so old
when he thought of all he had done in that time. No. He would not only go
with them, but he would be as agreeable as he could, if only to show himself that he was at last above that kind of thing.

Some human hearts are like a great ship that has no anchor, nor any means of making fast to moorings. The brave vessel sails through the stormy ocean, straining and struggling fiercely, till she lies at last within a fair harbour. But she has no anchor, and by and by the soft, smooth tide washes her out to sea, so gently and cruelly, out among the crests and the squalls and the rushing currents, and she must fain beat to windward again or perish on the grim lee shore.

Julius Batiscombe went to bed that night knowing that he was adrift, and yet denying it to himself; knowing that in a month, a week perhaps, he should be in trouble – in love – pah! how he hated the idea!

* * *

... [Leonora] had deceived herself into believing that she loved her husband, and the deception had cost her an effort. She was beginning to realise that the time was at hand when she might strive in vain to believe in her own sincerity, when her heart would not submit to any further equivocation, and when she should know in earnest what hollowness and weariness meant. As yet this was half unconscious, for it seemed so easy to make herself the injured party.

Poor Marcantonio was not to blame. He was the happiest of mortals, and went calmly on his way, doubting nothing and thinking that he was of all mortal men the most supremely fortunate.

Meanwhile Leonora kneeled in the rough little church, solacing herself with the catalogue of those ills she thought she was suffering. The stones were hard; there was a wretched little knot of country people, squalid and ill-savoured, who stared at the great lady for a moment, and then went on with their rosaries. A dirty little boy with a cane twenty feet long was poking a taper about and lighting lamps, and he dropped some of the wax on Leonora's gown. But she never shrank nor looked annoyed.

"All these things are very delightful," she said to herself, "if you only consider them as mortifications of the flesh."

She remembered how often just such little annoyances had sent her out of other churches disgusted and declaring that religion was a vain and hollow thing; and now, because she could bear with them and was not angry, she felt quite sure it was genuine.

"Yes," said she piously, as, an hour later, she picked her way home through the dusty road, "yes, the Church is a great refuge. I will go there every day."

Indeed, she was so resigned and subdued that evening at dinner, that Marcantonio asked whether she had a headache.

"Oh, no," she answered, "I am perfectly well, thank you."

"Because if you are indisposed, ma bien-aimée," continued her husband with some anxiety, "we will not go to Castellamare to-morrow."

"I will certainly go," she said. "I would go if I had twenty headaches," she might have added, for it would have been true.

"The occasion will be so much the more brilliant, ma très chère," remarked Marcantonio gallantly, as they went out into the garden under the stars.

"It is a hollow sham," said Leonora to herself. "He does not mean it."

But whether it was the effect of the morning, or the magic influence of Mr. Batiscombe's personality, is not certain; at all events when that gentleman appeared at the appointed hour to announce that his boat was in readiness, Leonora looked as though she had never known what care meant. She doubtless still remembered all she had thought on the previous afternoon, and she was still quite sure that her existence was a wreck and a misery, – but then, she argued, why should we poor misunderstood women not take such innocent pleasures as come in our way? It would be very wrong not to accept humbly the little crumbs of happiness, – and so on. So they went to Castellamare.

[Batiscombe's sailors row the party to the launching at Castellammare. In the course of an interminable ceremony, Leonora and Batiscombe chat with increasing nuance in English in front of the amiable Marcantonio, who does not understand that language.]

"I am afraid you will find this a dreadful bore," said Batiscombe to Leonora in English, while Marcantonio was busy trying to make out some of his friends on shore through a field-glass. Batiscombe had sat in the stern-sheets to steer during the trip, and having Leonora on one side of him and her husband on the other, had gone through an endless series of polite platitudes. If it had not been that Leonora attracted him so much he must himself have been bored to extinction. But then in that case he would probably not have put himself in such a position at all.

"Oh, nothing of this kind bores me," said Leonora cheerfully.

"You say that as though there were many kinds of things that did, though," observed Batiscombe, looking at her. It was a natural remark, without any intention.

"Dear me, yes!" exclaimed Leonora. "Life is not all roses, you know." She therewith assumed a thoughtful expression and looked away.

"I should not have supposed there were many thorns in your path, Marchesa. Would it be indiscreet to inquire of what nature they may be?"

Leonora was silent, and put up her glass to examine the proceedings on shore.

Batiscombe, who had come out that day with the sworn determination not to say or do anything to increase the interest he felt in the Marchesa, found himself wondering whether she were unhappy. The first and most natural conclusion was that she had been married to Marcantonio by designing parents, and that she did not care for him. Society said it had been a love-match, but what will society not say? "Poor thing," he thought, "I suppose she is miserable!"

"Forgive me," he said, in a low voice. "I did not know you were in earnest."

Leonora blushed faintly and glanced quickly at him. He had the faculty of saying little things to women that attracted their attention.

"What lots of poetry one might make about a launch," he said laughing, – for it was necessary to change the subject, – "ship – dip; ocean – motion; keel – feel; the rhymes are perfectly endless."

"Yes," said Leonora; "you might make a sonnet on the spot. Besides, there is a great deal of sentiment about the launching of a great man-of-war. The voyage of life – and that sort of thing – don't you know? How hot it is!"

"I will have another awning up in a minute," and he directed the sailors, helping to do the work himself. He stood upon the gunwale to do it.

"I am sure you will fall," said Leonora, nervously. "Do sit down!"

"If I had a millstone round my neck there would be some object in falling," said Batiscombe. "As it is, I should not even have the satisfaction of drowning."

"What an idea! Should you like to be drowned?" she said, looking up to him.

"Sometimes," he answered, still busy with the awning. Then he sat down again.

"You should not say that sort of thing," said Leonora. "Besides, it is rude to say you should like to be drowned when I am your guest."

"Great truths are not always pretty. But how could any man die better than at your feet?" He laughed a little, and yet his voice had an earnest ring to it. He had judged rightly when he foresaw that he must fall in love with Leonora.

Marcantonio, who did not understand English, was watching the proceedings on shore.

[When the launching ceremony finally ends, Batiscombe takes the

tiller and in a freshening wind the little craft heels over and begins the re-
turn to home.]

Batiscombe suggested that they should run into one of the great green caves that honeycomb the cliffs near Sorrento, and make it their dining-room. So away they went, rejoicing to be out of the heat and the noise. It was twelve o'clock, and far up among the orange groves the little church bells rang out their midday chime, laughing together in the white belfries for joy of the sunshine and the fair summer's day.

"I should like to be always sailing," said Leonora, who had now quite forgotten her woes and enjoyed the change.

"Ma chère," said her husband, "there is nothing simpler."

"You always say that," she answered rather reproachfully; "but this is the very first time I have been on the water since we came."

"My boat and my men are always at your disposal, Marchesa," said Batiscombe, looking down at her, "and myself, too, if you will condescend to employ me as your skipper."

"Thanks, you are very good," said she. "But I thought you were only passing, and were to be off in a few days?" She glanced up at him, as though she meant to be answered.

"Oh, it is very uncertain," said Batiscombe. "It depends," he added in a lower voice and in English, "upon whether you will use the boat." It was rather a bold stroke, but it told, and he was rewarded.

"I should like very much to go out again some day," she said.

Those little words and sentences, what danger signals they ought to be to people about to fall in love! Batiscombe knew it; he knew well that every such speech, in her native language and in a half voice, was one step nearer to the inevitable end. But he was fast getting to the point when, as far as he himself was concerned, the die would be cast. His manner changed perceptibly during the day, as the influence gained strength. His voice grew lower and he laughed less, while his eyes shone curiously, even in the mid-day sun.

The boat ran into the cave, which was the largest on the shore, and would admit the mast and the long yards without difficulty. Within the light was green, and the water now and again plashed on the rocks. The men steadied the craft with their oars and the party proceeded to lunch. Most of "society" has a most excellent appetite, and when one reflects how very hard society works to amuse itself, it is not surprising that it should need generous nourishment. The unlucky cook had done his best, and the result was satisfactory. There were all manner of things, and some bottles of strong Falerno wine. Batiscombe drank water and very little of it.

"Somebody has said," remarked Marcantonio with a laugh, "that one must distrust the man who drinks water when other people drink wine. We shall have to beware of you, Monsieur Batiscombe." He had learned the name very well by this time.

"Perhaps there is truth in it," said Batiscombe, "but it is not my habit I can assure you. The origin of the saying lies in the good old custom of doctoring other people's draughts. The man who drank water at a feast two hundred years ago was either afraid of being poisoned himself, or was engaged in poisoning his neighbours."

"Oh, the dear, good old time!" exclaimed Leonora, eating her salad daintily.

"Do you wish it were back again?" asked Batiscombe. "Are there many people you would like to poison?"

"Oh, not that exactly," and she laughed. "But life must have been very exciting and interesting then."

"Enfin," remarked Marcantonio, "I am very well pleased with it as it is. There was no opera, no election, no launching of war-ships; and when you went out you had to wear a patent safe on your head, in case anybody wanted to break it for you. And then, there was generally some one who did. Yes, indeed, it must have been charming, altogether ravishing. Allez! give me the nineteenth century."

"I assure you, Marchesa," said Batiscombe, "life can be exceedingly exciting and interesting now."

"I dare say," retorted Leonora, "for people who go round the world in boats in search of adventures, and write books abusing their enemies. But we – what do we ever do that is interesting or exciting? We stay at home and pour tea."

"And in those days," answered Batiscombe, "the ladies stayed at home and knit stockings, or if they were very clever they worked miles and miles of embroidery and acres of tapestry. About once a month they were allowed to look out of the window and see their relations beating each other's brains out with iron clubs, and running each other through the body with pointed sticks. As the Marchesa says, it was absolutely delightful, that kind of life."

"You are dreadfully prejudiced," said Leonora.

"But I am sure it was very nice."

And so they talked, and the men smoked a little, till they decided that they had had enough of it, and the oars plashed in the water together, sending the boat out again into the bright sun. In five minutes they were at the landing belonging to the Carantoni villa. There was a deep cleft in the cliffs just there, and the descent wound curiously in and out of the rock, so that in many places you could only trace it from below by the windows hewn in the solid stone to give light and air to the passage. The rocks ran out a little at the base, and there were steps carved for a landing. There are few places so strikingly odd as this landing to the Carantoni villa. Leonora said it was "eerie."

Everything prefigured in this passage – and more – does occur in the remainder of *To Leeward*.

Norman Douglas

Among the hundreds of people who were acquainted with Sorrento's famous adopted son, Marion Crawford, the Scottish writer Norman Douglas was one of the few who was not entranced by him. In the character sketch below, ostensibly about Crawford but also about himself, Douglas is straightforward about what he disliked in Crawford even as he acknowledges the man's undoubted accomplishments.

Given the many similarities between them – both were extraordinarily gifted men with compelling personalities – it may be that a tacit competitiveness colored their relationship. Douglas' family was aristocratic on both sides, the quarter-Austrian as well as the predominant Scottish. He was a born scholar and had been successful from the start in his academic pursuits. As a young man he held responsible posts in government service, including a two-and-a-half year stint at the British Embassy in Moscow as Third Secretary. He could have enjoyed a distinguished diplomatic career, but chose instead to turn to scholarship and writing. Crawford's youth, on the other hand, had not been nearly so focused or conventionally successful as Douglas', but it had been a lot more unconventional and his approach to learning had been through practical experiences.

Whatever the reasons in background and upbringing, Crawford and Douglas saw the world in radically different ways. Douglas' training as a scientist and wide learning undergird his individualistic prose. Crawford, on the other hand, was decidedly the Romantic moralist, absorbed by religious issues and devoted to the Roman Catholicism to which he had converted (as Douglas correctly guessed in his biographical sketch). Douglas' playful and vigorous prose may be more attractive to today's reader than Crawford's more mannered writing.

When a misunderstood incident caused him to lose his Scottish patrimony, Douglas too had to live more or less by his pen; in his sketch about Crawford, he describes how the American's example tempted him to try to make a living as a writer of Crawford-like fictions, with laughable results. His real genius as a writer, as the remaining sections show, was in the kind of prose musings – wide ranging and provocative – that complete this chapter. His *Siren Land* is perhaps *the* classic appreciation of the Sorrentine peninsula.

NORMAN DOUGLAS, "Mr Marion Crawford" from *Looking Back* (1933)

Those "breadcrust bombs," as Johnston-Lavis calls them, were ejected from the crater of Vulcano in 1888 and are of different sizes; some reach the height of a man, others will go into your pocket. They lie scattered over the surrounding country and also, unfortunately for me (as it turned out), under the surface of the ground. You stride down the cone of Vulcano, which consists of ashes and cinders, as you stride down that of Vesuvius – with seven-league boots; as fast as you like, and sinking deeply into the soft material with every step. This is what I was doing when my foot encountered an underground obstacle. It was one of those infernal bombs. Straightway the ankle was twisted, and with such violence that I actually thought to hear it crack. It may have been imagination. The pain was real.

That crawl down to the beach where my boat was waiting – for I had to return to the main island of Lipari, as the Narlians' house on Vulcano had not yet been re-built after its shattering – that crawl, in the glowing heat of midday, has not been forgotten. The ground was trackless and so rough that I soon found it easiest to go on all fours over the hot stones. Arrived at the shore, I relieved the pain by dangling my foot in the water till we reached Lipari.

Later on my chief amusement was to hobble down to the harbour on two sticks and watch the life there. A newcomer had arrived one morning, a Sorrentine felucca, and on her deck stood a sailorly man who hailed me in English. "I'm Marion Crawford," he said...

Afterwards I saw more of him, staying sometimes in Sorrento at their home overlooking the sea on that cliff, that precarious tufa-cliff which he presently faced with an expensive buttress of hewn lava, whereon may be read the inscription "In Tempestate Securitas." An enormous glycinia trailed over half the garden, and in its shade might be seen pieces of marble statuary lying about. These were the work of Crawford's father, the sculptor of whom Nathaniel Hawthorne makes fun in one of his books.

I often wondered what induced Crawford – what induces any one – to live at Sorrento. It is damp and unhealthy in winter; it looks west, and during the long summer days there is no escaping from that wretched sun till it sets. As to landscape – even the profile of Vesuvius, whose beauty would seem to be indestructible, takes on an ugly shape at Sorrento. The inhabitants are nowise to my taste, and if they complain that foreigners now go there less frequently they have only themselves to blame – their harassing beggars, guides, coachmen, touts of every kind. Some of these nuisances are being abated. They cannot abate this one, that there are no country walks to be taken except between high walls. You are confined to a villa or hotel garden, or to a boat on the sea. They charge you seven francs for a whisky-and-soda (in Capri you pay four and a half), and dole out the stuff reluctantly, drop by drop, as if they were selling you liquid gold.

There was a good library in Crawford's house. Here you could browse in peace. In this room he had lately written his novels – one a year, he told me. *Khaled* was his favourite among them, and only a single one, he said, showed the faintest tinge of impropriety (? *To Leeward*); he had never ceased to regret the publication of that book. He cruised about in summer, lectured for three months in America, his native country, and passed a few days every year in London discussing business with his publisher Macmillan. He told me that he would not allow his wife to set foot in England. He bore a grudge against that country and spoke with bitterness of "the Anglo-Saxon"; Scotsmen, he explained, were not included under that term. I never discovered his reason for this fad. Maybe it originated in some unpleasant experience of his own with a representative of the Anglo-Saxon race; maybe it was due to the behaviour of that monster Henry the Eighth. For Crawford, like other people, had his cloven hoof. He was a fine example of the water-tight compartment system.

A many-sided man, a linguist, scholar, and traveller, Crawford had a genuine passion for exploring byways ethnographical and philological; there was no question about that. Then came the cloven hoof. After some sensible or even profound remark on Buddhism or a quite dispassionate review of the origin of religions in general, he would utter one or two flaming ineptitudes about "Our Lady." He was a rabid Catholic. This militant pre-possession infects certain of his books, and when Ouida, in her early and well-balanced critique of them, says that "he must clear his mind of cobwebs, and he must realize that the 'unbelievers' and revolutionists, who at present horrify him, constitute the keenest intellectual element in Italy, indeed, the only healthy one," she lets him off almost too easily for trying to thrust his antediluvian bigotry down the reader's throat.

One sometimes wonders why northern Catholics and especially converts – was Crawford a convert? I think his father was – one wonders why these people are so obtrusive in their professions of faith. The religion of Chaucer's England was unobtrusive, unconstrained. It must have been the Reformation which gave a note of self-consciousness to the older faith, whose adherents now found themselves in the minority and surrounded by an alien creed; and it is natural that converts from Protestantism should resent this state of affairs more acutely than Catholics by birth. Hence their exacerbation. No southerners I ever met have talked about religion in the style of Crawford; they might be the devoutest believers, and yet they could not help smiling at what he said and how he said it. He was fatuously concerned about what, to them, are commonplaces.

Some trouble would have been avoided if Catholicism had never strayed beyond the Mediterranean basin. There, rooted in that old paganism – there is its home. Transalpine Catholicism lacks the historical roots of the other; it is no indigenous growth but a graft, for those particular pre-Christian cults are not our heritage. That is one difference between the two. Another is that Papal Rome takes the mysteries and dogmas of its creed with an easy grace and lightheartedness which, even before the Reformation, was not to be found in dour countries of the North. And that creed was at its most mellow and urbane stage of development when officious hyperborean boors like Luther began to meddle with it, and to invent a modified brand which was bound to end in reaction and the appearance of types like Crawford, who was more Catholic than the Pope. Always meddling! Somebody, one of these days, must be good enough to write a short sketch of the chief meddlers who have afflicted mankind, meddlers spiritual and also temporal – Julius Caesar, Napoleon...

There is another defect in Crawford's romances, and in many recent ones as well. I mean the interjection of remarks by the author, speaking in the first person. Crawford, having conducted you with the skill of a born story-teller into some historical or imaginary situation, proceeds to offer you, *à propos de bottes,* his individual opinion on the question (say) of divorce. Bad art! Such an intrusion is a jar. It spoils the flow of the story, its verisimilitude, its *tonalité.* If a writer can compress his views on divorce into an epigrammatic form he may put them into the mouth of one of his characters, or into a supposed train of reflection pursued by that character; if not, then the place for such observations is an article in some paper or a public platform. Altogether, there is careless work in the make-up of these novels. There was careless work in the make-up of Crawford himself. You heard a discordant note now and then, despite his fine presence, his intelligence, and that lustrous Vatican-society veneer. I will not say that a North-American Catholic is as disquieting a phenomenon as a Japanese Jew, but the way Crawford could talk about the money he made and the aristocratic friends he possessed was sometimes suggestive of a *rastaquero*. I daresay we all have our vulgar moments...

In July 1897 I went for a short cruise with him and some of his family in the *Alda*. This was not the Sorrentine felucca of long ago but an American pilot-boat, which he had fitted up comfortably and sailed himself across the Atlantic (he held a Master Mariner's Certificate from the Board of Trade: another attainment). We were away for the better part of a month, touching at Corsica, Elba, some of the smaller Tyrrhenian islands, Porto San Stefano and Città Vecchia. From there Crawford and myself went to Rome where he wanted to show me something; on our return we had a look at Gaeta and its "Montagna Spaccata," of which he told me the pious legend. Then we rejoined the *Alda* at Gaeta and he dropped me at Baiae. Out of sheer joy at the thought of being definitely on land once more I walked the whole way home to the Posilipo over Pozzuoli, sending my luggage with the carriage which should have conveyed my person.

Of the watery part of that trip I remember only that one day, because it happened to be Crawford's birthday, I imprudently drank his health in white wine. That scared him; it would bring bad luck, he vowed; I must drown it in red – which I did, and even so he was not quite happy. We also ran into a raging summer squall of the kind which was responsible for Shelley's death – a momentary blackness and welter, with lightning at close quarters.

At this period I already began to see a financial cataclysm looming ahead, and was casting about for some means of staving it off. Here was Crawford, producing an enviable income with one novel a year. Why not follow his example?

We had made our longest stay, eight or ten days, in the secluded harbour of Porto Longone on Elba. This gave me an opportunity of exploring the island in many directions, even to distant places like S. Ilario and Marciana. My favourite walk in the near neighbourhood was up a glen at the head of which stood a shrine dedicated to the Virgin of Monserrato; a lonesome spot. I had made friends with the Porto Longone priest, who showed me one day the parochial archives. Here I discovered a sensational entry in Latin. Thus it runs:

"Die 15 Martii I692. Bernardinus Mellini a Terra Rivi [now called Rio] huius insulae Ilvae, Eremita Bmae Virginis Montis Serrati huius Territorii, fuit inventus occisus decollatus in cella Eremitorii; cuius cadaver fuit sepultum in sepultura Ecclesiae Bmae Virginis Carmelitanae per Rm. D.

Michaelem Solimenum ex commissione mei Parr. Lazari Bartoli"... in short, on the 15 March 1692 the hermit of this sanctuary of Monserrato was found dead and beheaded in his cell – murdered, presumably, by some person or persons unknown. Round this, the slaughter of a seventeenth-century anchorite in his solitary retreat among the rocks, could be woven a romance, an intrigue of love and revenge.

After consulting many books on Elba and its history for purpose of local colour I made a "romance" out of it which still exists, and which will not exist much longer. It is called *A Tale of Elba*. The manuscript, in 103 closely-written folio pages, is over-crowded with subsequent erasures and corrections which testify to a laudable zeal for improvement and, at the same time, to a lamentable thoughtlessness, for the alterations are so thickly strewn that it is hard to discover the right text. Not that it matters! The tale is contemporary with the life of the hero – of the hermit, that is, who was killed in mysterious circumstances in 1692 and whom I convert into a Spaniard. It suffers from a fatal blemish. The action is retrospective; it consists of voluminous reflections, a kind of memoir, written by the hermit. This blunts the dramatic edge. There is a love-element in the person of Beatrice, an Etruscan background (Elba was a dependency of Volterra), a Spanish infusion, a voyage to Sicily, a dwarf, the gardener Isidoro, a Corsair raid, a French attack on Porto Longone, the iron mines of the neighbouring Rio, a Peruvian emerald, "the shining green jewel that was set in a ring which Dona Maria brought with her from countries where her father had fought under Pizarro," an ominous and oft-repeated reference to the Ides of March, the day on which the hero, who has sinned in his youth, awaits his destruction at the hands of the Avenger, Brother Martin.

(Page 2) "...I write in my cell at night. It is bitter cold among these moist rocks; although March has begun, the spring refuses to visit this dank and shady cleft. It is the fated year 1692. Why fated? I shall tell anon. And I am old – old and grey. The Destroyer has never left me for fifty odd years. Fifty years of terror, of broken slumbers, humiliation, dread. And my hands are stained with innocent blood. I am become a murderer, desperate of salvation. And he, the Avenger, knows all and waits, and waits... he waits for the Ides of March...." (Page 95) "...But have a care, my friend, how you cross a despairing man. This life of doubt must now end, and if you approach me with evil intentions... You are younger than myself and somewhat taller, but I will fight like the mountain cat, for seventy years have not dimmed my sight and my muscles are yet supple...."

That was the style: a tiresome monologue.

NORMAN DOUGLAS, *Siren Land* (1911)

From Chapter II: *The Uplands of Sorrento*

... Neapolitans have grown rich again and seek the fine air of the hills as of yore, while the inhabitants themselves bring much money from New York; and from Argentina, where a good half of them are periodically employed in selling potatoes to the Spaniards, who apparently eat nothing else. "Good people" they call them, because they are easily gulled in the matter of weights and measures.

One consequence of this revival is that the price of land is rising once more and new houses are being built. This would be satisfactory, were it not that the style of architecture has changed for the worse. That harmonious medley of small vaulted chambers with their vine-shaded loggia in front, so becoming to this climate and charming to look upon, has been displaced by hideous *palazzi* constructed with iron beams, asphalt, and roofing tiles – things formerly unheard of. No person with a sense of the fitness of things will ever fall in love with these new dwellings, although they are built, as the architects will tell you, according to the latest *regola d'arte*. When a Southerner discourses upon *regola d'arte*, he is generally up to some mischief.

Even the colossal hand-made house-keys of the olden days, now replaced by weedy cast-iron abominations, were not without a certain austere beauty: there was a smack of Saint Peter about them. And they had their uses, too. Three years ago a wealthy landowner, returning home at night, was attacked by two ruffians with knives. Having no ordinary weapon of defence, not even a walking-stick, he began to wield his house-key with such dexterity that one of his assailants was brained on the spot, while the other crawled into the fields, where he was found dead next morning – at least, he ought to have been.

The ridge of backbone which divides the gulfs of Salerno and Naples is called *Le Tore...*

It is not a crest but a rounded plateau, and as the divide approaches far nearer to the southern shore, the rocks on this incline needs must rush precipitously into the sea, with perilous paths into grottos, and thrifty olives on the middle heights grasping the limestone ledges or climbing warily down the gullies; the northern slope, on which Massa and Sorrento lie, is a gentle declivity planted with vines and oranges and walnuts, and refreshed by streams that run through the heat of the dog-days. The Tore reach their highest elevation immediately behind Sorrento. Here, in the early morning, when sea-mists on either side shroud the two gulfs from view, the wanderer has all the illusion of being on some lonely Alpine meadow – not a sign of human habitation or handiwork; a chill nip in the air; browsing cattle with deep-toned bells round their necks, and real, close-cropped turf under foot. This, I imagine, is the track which the wolves follow when they leave their fastnesses of the Sant' Angelo in winter to scour the richer country.

... This is essentially a land of line, of irreproachable contours, and your painter had best begin by throwing away his palette and striving to see it aright: a land of classical parsimony, limestone and blue sea, whose chastened beauty none save a really great craftsman, with disciplined hand and heart attuned to eternal melodies, can hope to disentangle from among the prejudices and traditions of his own mind. What caricatures are the works of even world-famous artists who have painted on these shores; what faulty draughtsmanship, meretricious effects, and lack of decent restraint! How they fail to see the simplicity underlying those complex natural formations! For the loveliness of this landscape is not that of Phryne, and the painter errs who thinks that his inmost thoughts are met half-way by a smile of encouragement. The smile is there, but not for him. It is for the constraining mortal who disregards it; who stands to his work in the relation of God to man.

...

... The landscape, ... and not only the hour and the man, plays a part when gods are to be created. Perhaps this helps us to understand the enigma of universal Pan. From being an Arcadian forest-god he became, as culture advanced, diffused and impalpable. The forest lost its noonday mystery and its Embodiment was no longer seen of men; he was merged into the brooding meridian stillness of all earth which no clearings, no cornfields, no sparkling cities could impair; his weaker comrades, the fauns and dryads, unable to endure this searching light, took refuge in yet shadier groves, or pined away.

Nor do immortal gods look down from cloudy pavilions, for the sky here is a vast dome, and not a plane. Wherever thunder-clouds touch mountain summits this quaint belief will arise, and Zeus, whatever his origin, found a congenial home in Greece, where the exhalations, formerly more abundant, even now repose upon the hill-tops. In Siren land they do not; they sail overhead in summer-time, a painted argosy that seldom anchors to spill its dewy freight against the mountain-sides, though the *Cloud-gatherer* – when the south wind blows – is busy as at Aegina, collecting out of a sunny sea invisible wreaths of vapour...

...

... To dream in Siren land, pursuing the moods and memories as they shift in labyrinthine mazes, like shadows on a woodland path in June; to stroll among the hills and fill the mind with new images upon which to browse at leisure, casting off outworn weeds of thought with the painless ease of a serpent and unperplexing, incidentally, some of those "questions of the day" of which the daily papers nevertheless know nothing – this is an antidote for many ills. There is repose in Siren land; there is none of that delirious massing-together in which certain mortals, unable to stand alone, can lean up against one another and so gain, for a moment, a precarious condition of equipoise.

From Chapter XIII: *The Headland of Minerva*

There is a project afoot to continue the driving-road from Sorrento, which now ends at Termini, as far as the point of Campanella. Italy is full of such designs of local patriotism. Often enough, after some thoughtful mayor has collected money during his term of office for an undertaking of this kind – roads, drainage, or water-supply – his successor will spend the whole sum in pyrotechnics in honour of the village saint: thousands of francs carefully hoarded up being thus thrown away in a wild orgy of a single night. Shoulders are shrugged; a new collection begun: *Italia farà da sè* – that charming mixture of enthusiasm and inefficiency! It will ever be thus under a communal system as established here; no public spirit can exist where the good intentions of a few are absorbed by the vices to which the institution lends itself; where each reacts upon the other by ties of relationship or business and by preordained obligations of love and hatred; where the caprice or envy of a single man will suffice to frustrate a project secretly approved by all. What they require, these villages, is an independent and benevolent tyrant after the pattern of the old *podestà*: the municipal system marks a theory of government which ill accords with their habits of life.

Not that the building of this road is a pressing need. There are too many roads in the country already and, were nothing else to be amended, I could wish that the inhabitants might long continue to waste their superfluous wealth in making noises and bad smells to the glory of God – for such are the local fireworks.

...

If you are in the mood for a scramble, you can be rowed from Campanella a mile in the Massa direction as far as the Cala di Mitigliano, and thence climb up the ravine to the summit of Mount San Costanzo. It is rough walking till the farm of Mitigliano, about half-way, is reached. In the vineyards here may be seen a few Roman remains and four huge amphorae, one of them still intact and in its original position. This, then, is the ancient Metellianum (there is another place of this name near Cava). And not far from this site were unearthed, some six years ago, a "shepherd" of gold and a metal helmet which were sold for fifty francs to a Sorrento jeweller, though "who knows how many millions they were really worth." It is impossible to obtain clear details of such discoveries; not only are the natives incapable of describing what they see with their eyes, but also, like the Irish, they hesitate to reply until they know what one would be glad to hear; if one persists in merely asking for the truth, they suspect hidden motives and become evasive. The Oriental influence, I suppose – the same which always prompts them to answer one question with another.

"Why do you invariably answer my questions with another question?" I once enquired.

"Why shouldn't I?"

... And everywhere the unharvested sea. The sea, with its intense restfulness, is the dominant note of Siren land. There is no escaping from it. Incessant gleams of light flash from that mirror-like expanse; even when unperceived by the senses, among squalid tenements or leafy uplands, they will find you out and follow, like some all-pervading, inevitable melody. How the *Odyssey* throbs with those luminous vibrations! Forest voices are the music of Bach; we seem to wander in cool wooded glades with sunlight pouring through leaves overhead, to breathe the fragrance of dew-spangled moss and fern, to hear the caress of light winds playing among the crowns and the rustling of branches and streamlets and all those elfish woodland notes which the master himself, in his solitary wanderings, had heard and thenceforth emprisoned everlastingly – coaxing their echoes into those numbers whose enchantment none but chosen spirits, little less than angels, can unseal. Some are of multiple voice, like that god-gifted Tschaikovsky, whose melancholy is flecked by exotic passions such as Mozart or Beethoven never sang – for how shall that come out of a man which was never in him? – lilting, super-sensuous measures from old Samarkand where they loved with the love of daemons; muffled pulsations, oft-repeated, doom-enforcing; or an ominous metallic quaver – the wail of the myriad Tartars who fell by the blood-stained waters of Tengis, or, it may be, some premonitory cry of his own tormented soul that fled from earth, all too soon.

... There are many spots on earth as fair as the Parthenopean bay – equally fair at least to us moderns, whose appreciation of art and of nature has become less exclusively human. The steaming Amazonian forests and the ice-crags of Jan Mayen appeal since yesterday to our catholic taste; but whoever takes the antique point of view will still accord the palm to the Mediterranean. Here, true beauty resides with its harmony of form and hue – here the works of man stand out in just relation to those of nature, each supplementing the other. Elsewhere, she is apt to grow menacing – gloomy or monstrous. In the North, the sun refuses her aid and man struggles with the elements; he vegetates, an animated lump of blubber and dirt, or rushes frantically in starving hordes to overrun the bright places of earth; in the tropics his works shrink into insignificance, he is lost in a fierce tangle of greenery, sucked dry by the sun, whom he execrates as a demon – he dwindles into a stoic, a slave. Here, too, an ancient world, our ancient world, lies spread out in rare charm of colour and outline, and every footstep is fraught with memories. The lovely islands of the Pacific have a past, but their past is not our past, and men who strike deep notes in such alien soil are like those who forsake their families and traditions to live among gipsies. Niagara will astound the senses, but the ruins of Campania wake up sublimer and more enduring emotions.

No person of culture, however prosaic, will easily detach himself from such scenes and thoughts – is it not the prerogative of civilized man to pause and ponder before the relics of his own past?

It is time to depart. The swallows have flown overhead on their long journey, and the redbreast's plaintive whistle announces that the summer is ended.

And how much there is still to see – the remains of Pollio's temple with the baths of Queen Joan, and crumbling towers and sites innumerable! Yonder is Erche, for instance – a commanding plateau opposite Santa Maria surrounded by ravines on three sides and within a few hundred yards of which the old Roman road to Minerva's temple must have passed: how came the name of Hercules to wander so far inland? And only the other day I found my way to a solitary group of houses called Scuola, a singular appellation which reminds me of that *school* of poets and philosophers which was imagined to lie near the promontory of Athenaeum; the Sirens' songs, according to Pontanus, being nothing but the irresistible seduction of eloquence and literary pursuits. "What has been said of the sweet voices and songs of the Sirens is a fable illustrating the attractions of eloquence, and the cult of knowledge of letters." Was it not good of the old humanist to associate the Sirens with lettered ease? At Scuola, too, there stands a decayed chapel with a pavement of hand-painted tiles that depict the expulsion of our first parents from Paradise. They shine with the lustre of eternal youth and, to judge by the date, the work may well have been executed by the hand of the celebrated Lionardo Chiaiese who, together with his two brothers, was a pioneer of majolica in Naples, and whose two other pavements, at Anacapri and in the Neapolitan nunnery of Suor Orsola Benincasa, are considered masterpieces impossible to reproduce with modern methods. The scene is drawn with great freedom and taste, and I have endeavoured, twice, to interest certain folks at Naples to safeguard it ere the crazy roof, through which green plants are vigorously sprouting, shall crash down upon the stern young archangel and all the wondrous beasts of the garden.

It is the same everywhere. Go where you will, new discoveries and suggestions are lying in wait; impossible to avoid stumbling upon relics of Roman rule, of old Hellas, or mediaeval romance that are crowded into these few miles. The memories start up at our feet, like the fabled dragon-brood of Cadmus. These are the delights of Siren land.

But the summer is ended, though there may well be another kind of Siren land where we can take our joy at all seasons, if so disposed. Not in the stars, however: nobody but Plato would have thought of making the Sirens live in those remote spheres. What you cannot find on earth is not worth seeking.

CHAPTER 7

REVOLUTIONARIES IN PARADISE

Visitors to Sorrento come because of the beauty and the attractions. But some find in Sorrento an ideal place to get away from the distractions of home. Such was the case for Henrik Ibsen (1828-1906), Maksim Gorky (1868-1936), and Isaac Babel (1894-1941), who gave scant attention to Sorrento itself. Instead, they used their tenancy in paradise to focus themselves on their real concerns. Living in the sun, Ibsen drew a bead on the dark, oppressive social climate of nineteenth-century Norway. Gorky was deeply involved in the violent social and political upheavals of early twentieth-century Russia but needed distance to produce well. Babel found in Sorrento a necessary respite from increasingly difficult days in the Soviet Union in 1933.

The three writers knew that they could work better away from home. Life was quieter, there were fewer distractions, irritating worries could be left behind. They feared, with reason, getting caught up in the activities and intrigues of their respective societies. For the Russians, there was always also the very real worry of getting dangerously involved in an unexpected political spasm at home that might have serious personal consequences for them.

So focused were all three writers on their own countries and problems that they made only the most passing references to Sorrento in their letters and diaries. Ibsen says almost nothing directly about the stunning meeting of cliff and sea outside his Hotel Tramontano windows, for instance. Gorky likes the conditions of life in Sorrento, and says so, but scarcely effusively. He may have been a bit jaded: he had spent seven years in Capri before later coming to Sorrento. But Isaac Babel, newly arrived in 1933 for the autumn and winter, stops to take an appreciative if brief look at his new location: "The earthly paradise, I suppose, must look about like the Capo di Sorrento."

Henrik Ibsen

In his daily life, the Norwegian playwright Henrik Ibsen seemed a conventional, stuffy sort of man. But he thought and wrote like a revolutionary. In play after play he laid bare the hypocrisy beneath the staid Victorian veneer of contemporary Scandinavian society. His works enjoyed enormous publicity – notoriety – throughout Europe and the United States and even today they are widely read, frequently performed, and still capable of shocking.

Ibsen seemed to need distance from his targets to take better aim at them. He spent most of his productive years in self-imposed exile from Norway. Some of his earlier works are set at least partly in non-Scandinavian locales, for instance *Peer Gynt* (based on the exploits of the Norwegian folk hero), whose final two acts were composed during Ibsen's 1867 stay in Sorrento, at the time of an unusually torrid scirocco. Ibsen had been staying on the island of Ischia when a mild earthquake drove him, always averse to risk, to find more firm surroundings. He ended up in Sorrento for two months. He revisited Sorrento very briefly in 1878, then for a longer period, to finish *Ghosts* (1881).

The great plays of Ibsen's maturity are set in gloomy Norwegian drawing rooms. But they were written in sunny, spacious lands far from Scandinavia. Ibsen was always on the move. He preferred large apartments (like the one at the Hotel Tramontano in 1881), so that he could pace back and forth between three or four rooms. Larger relocations were part of the picture, too. He would place the heavy weight of a writing project on himself, labor to finish it, then flee to elsewhere, where he would begin the process all over again. *A Doll's House* (1879) was written in southern Italy, as was *An Enemy of the People* (1882). *Ghosts* (1881) is probably Ibsen's most revolutionary play. It was composed largely in Sorrento. It could not, in Ibsen's own mind, have been written in Norway. In a letter of 15 October 1876 to his mother-in-law, Ibsen analyzes the daily conditions of Norwegian life. "I often wonder how you can endure them yourself. Life there, as it presents itself to me now, has something indescribably wearisome about it; it wearies the soul out of one, wearies the strength out of one's will. That is the accursed thing about small surroundings – they make the soul small."

Plaque celebrating Henrik Ibsen's sojourn at the Hotel Tramontano

The *Ghosts* in the title of Ibsen's famous play are those worn-out conventions of middle-class life that make a society dishonest, and that come back to haunt it. Helene Alving, the main character, tries to spare her son the ugliness of Scandinavian life, aiming above all to shelter him from the knowledge that his father was a dissolute man. She sends the boy to Paris and maintains the myth of Captain Alving's saintliness. In Paris Oswald discovers a real joy in life. But now he has returned to Norway, in the final stages of syphilis. Oswald believes that his syphilis must somehow have been caused by the pure delight he took in living in the sunny south. Although a doctor had told him that the syphilis was congenital, Oswald refuses the explanation – it can't be, his father was a saint! After all, his mother told him so. Knowing that insanity is close upon him, Oswald asks his mother to give him poison when he loses his mind. At the play's end, Oswald descends into madness.

The name of the town Sorrento appears almost nowhere in Ibsen's works, except in the datelines of a handful of letters, some parts of which appear below. However, when doomed diseased Oswald begs, "The sun... Mother, give me the sun," he is not only invoking the play's central image. The sun *is* the joy in life that he (like his creator) found so elusive in gloomy Norway. Even more, the image shows Ibsen's deep debt to Sorrento's brilliantly bright days, the clear air and soaring elevations that let him see so far, so clearly.

The first of these letters was written during the period Ibsen was finishing the play *Peer Gynt*. The second comments on the oppressive heat of August, 1881, and the third reveals that although the heat was enough to curtail walking, it could not stop Ibsen from soldiering on with *Ghosts*.

HENRIK IBSEN, *The Correspondence* (1905)

From Letter 42. *To Magdalene Thoresen*

Sorrento, 15th October 1867

I congratulate you most heartily upon Sara's marriage. Please give her my best wishes. I am really glad on her account that her home is to be in Copenhagen, as I do not think her particularly fitted for the conditions of life in Norway. If there is any disparagement in this remark, it applies to the conditions, and not to her. I often wonder how you can endure them your-self. Life there, as it presents itself to me now, has something indescribably wearisome about it; it wearies the soul out of one, wearies the strength out of one's will. That is the accursed thing about small surroundings – they make the soul small.

It will not be long, I imagine, before Dorothea, too, leaves home; and then you will not be so tied down.* You ought to, and must, come to Italy; and you must not make a rush through the country, but a considerable stay in it...

I cannot tell very much about my travels in a letter. We went to Ischia about the middle of May, and stayed there until the middle of August; since then we have been moving from one place to another on the southern side of the bay, manoeuvering to escape cholera, etc. At the end of this month we go back to Rome. The Papal States are, as you probably know, in revolt, and we should like to see a little of what is going on.

I have completed a new dramatic poem, which is to be published at Christmas; it will greatly interest me to know what you think of it. It is called *Peer Gynt,* after the chief character, about whom a little is told in As-björnsen's book of fairy-tales. I had not much to build upon, but have con-sequently been able to deal the more freely with the subject, according to my own requirements.

I learn from Hegel that your new book is not to be published until spring, and that it will be a big one. This is all that we know about it; but I am looking forward to it with pleasureable eagerness. One advantage, at least, we reap from living abroad – the national life comes to us from home purged and in extract; we are spared what goes on in the streets and lanes, and are gainers thereby. We have not seen any Norwegian newspapers of later date than the beginning of May.

From Letter 153. *To Camilla Collett*

Sorrento, August 1881

... My wife suffers more than we *[his adult son Sigurd and Ibsen himself]* do from the heat, and especially from the sirocco; but she manages to keep in health by bathing every day. I do not believe that you could have stood a whole summer down here. Walking is almost out of the question; one has to keep as still as possible.

---

* Magdalene Thoresen was the mother of Susanna, Ibsen's wife. Sara and Dorothea were Magdalene's daughters by her second husband and thus Susanna's half-sisters.

From Letter 154. *To Ludwig Passarge*

Sorrento, 17th August 1881

I am engaged this summer in writing a new play, which will appear in autumn, and which I shall then have the pleasure of sending you.

This play was, of course, *Ghosts*, which feels far distant from Sorrento but which couldn't have been written anywhere else.

Maksim Gorky

A tireless writer and social activist, Maksim Gorky was born and raised in Russia, considered himself a Russian patriot, and died in his motherland. But he spent many long periods abroad. During the whole of Gorky's life, Russia was wracked with internal strife including the revolution against the Czars. Gorky involved himself actively in the political events of his day and also wrote powerfully about life in society's "lower depths." For his efforts he was frequently under surveillance by Czarist police, and later by various post-revolutionary factions. He beat a prudent retreat abroad on many occasions, with long-term tenancy first in Capri and later in Sorrento.

MAKSIM GORKY, *Selected Letters* (1997)

There is no doubt that Gorky enjoyed the conditions of daily life in Sorrento. His letter to a friend after first setting up his household there shows his appreciation, as well as his characteristic ironic humor.

From Letter 114. *To Petr Petrovich Kruichkov*

5 May 1924

We are living quite tolerably here; they treat us with affection and care, and give us food and drink – but they do still take money for it all the same. And I had thought...

We have rented a house on a bluff overlooking the sea; if an earthquake should occur, we would be the first to tumble into the water. The house is old but comfortable, with some fourteen rooms – yes! There is of course a room for you; we are expecting you. And what a garden! Palm trees, grapes, and oranges. They've taken about 500 dollars from us for all this until 15 November. A pretty penny! But we have complete isolation and even our own beach! We haven't moved yet. The move won't affect the address; it remains Sorrento, M. Gorki.

Excellent weather has set in; the sea is calm, and the sun and other heavenly bodies are toiling honestly, albeit without pay. I am hardly coughing at all, but I am beginning to suspect that the germs have switched apartments, moving from my lungs to my bowels. Well, never mind that! Germs want to live too. I am feeding myself on fish. Now and then I go for walks and boat trips. But there is an awful amount of work; manuscripts and more manuscripts!...

Gorky continued to live in the house he described to Petr Petrovich for all the years of his stay in Sorrento, with various Russian expatriates like himself as guests. Yet he apparently felt a bit guilty about its splendors. He took pains to downplay them when he replied to a letter accusing him of living inappropriately well for a revolutionary.

Letter 158. *To Popov* *

3 January 1931

You wrote me a very good letter, Comrade Popov. I did not find any "sharp words" in it; however, I did gain a clear sense of its sincerity and forthrightness. I will answer you in the same manner that you wrote to me.

As far as the villa is concerned, you've been misled. I have never owned one, I do not own one now, and of course I shall never own one in the future either. I am quite incapable of lying, and it would be a great lie if I were to acquire property at a time when I am rejoicing at the mighty task of building socialism by the working class of the Union of Soviets. I would do far better in terms of the "acquisition of every comfort" – i.e. the facilities which my age, my work, and my state of health demand – were I to reside in the Soviet Union and not here. I am not having my sons educated in "bourgeois schools"; I have one son only, and he is my secretary. He is thirty years old and married with two children; they are too young to be going to school yet. It is the bourgeois *émigré* press which has foisted this "villa" and "comfort" upon me, and it has done so with a simple aim, which is to compromise me in the eyes of sincere but credulous socialists.

In the Union of Soviets there are, of course, places no worse than Sorrento, but, if I were to live over there, I would live in Moscow. It would make no sense for me to live on the Black Sea, for instance; that's almost as far from Moscow as Italy is. And in Moscow there would be meetings, visits of various sorts, and so on, all of which would interfere with my work.

Here I live in total isolation and alone; and this allows me to work in tranquillity for ten or twelve hours a day. In Moscow I would be tempted to go to the theatre and take trips hither and thither; whereas over here I never go to the theatre, and it's even been two months since I last went into town, which is only three kilometers from my apartment.

The "Italian censorship" cannot cause me any hindrance. I have always written what I know and what I think "without caution." There is no reason for them to "arrest" me, and if I were to be arrested, it would cause a scandal which could only be of value to our cause in the Union of S[ocialist] S[oviets]. So there you have it, my dear fellow!

All the same, I will be coming back to live in the Soviet Union; the times are such that one needs to be at home.

But I will move only after I've finished all the work I have begun here. I shall visit [Russia] again this year, though, in April.

Does my answer satisfy you? If not, then do write to me again and I'll answer.

Thank you for the letter. A very good letter it was too.

Warm regards,

A. Peshkov

* Popov (his other names are unknown) was a factory worker from Leningrad who had written to Gorky complaining of the comfortable life the writer was leading 'in Fascist Italy' and asking him to settle in the Soviet Union. [Editors' note in Maksim Gorky, *Selected Letters*.]

The fourteen-room house has shrunk to an apartment in this rendering. And when Gorky denies owning a villa he is technically correct (he rented it), but perhaps a little misleading. There is no doubt, however, that he did work indefatigably, in Sorrento as everywhere (it is said that his lifetime output of letters alone exceeded 20,000). And he was certainly aware of how crucial freedom from outside complications was to his production as a writer.

From Letter 131. *To F. V. Gladkov*

30 November 1926

I live in Italy because, were I to live in Russia, I would never get any work done; I would simply travel from city to city, go from house to house and – chat. And – certainly, inevitably – I would quarrel bitterly with many different people, especially with the literary critics...

It is not surprising that Gorky should have written sparingly about Sorrento's delights – that would have been politically imprudent. Then too, he was an old-timer in paradise, having lived in Capri for seven years before he set up his even longer-term tenancy in Sorrento.

Maksim Gorky was born Alexey Maksimovich Peshkov. When he published his first story, in 1892, he assumed the pen name under which the world now knows him. *Gorky* means *bitter* in Russian, and bitter indeed was young Alexey Maksimovich's sense of his country's injustices. Bitter too his own early experiences. Alexey's parents had married over her father's violent opposition. Three years after Alexey's birth his parents and the boy moved away, to a port city where Gorky's father found a responsible position. The family enjoyed a brief period of stable prosperity, but Gorky's father died of cholera when the boy was four years old. His younger brother died a few weeks later as the children and their mother were making their way back to her family home. Varvara never recovered from the trauma of her double loss; she essentially abandoned her surviving child and drifted farther and farther away from him and from reality.

Meanwhile, Varvara's parents' fortunes were rapidly deteriorating, and they slipped from their eminence as prosperous dye merchants to end up as declassed beggars. The decline exacerbated his grandfather's always violent temper and the old man increasingly took out his rage on whoever was closest. At the age of not quite eleven, Alexey was thrown out of his grandparents' house to fend for himself. His grandfather had given him one important gift, however – he had taught the boy to read. Alexey's love of literature saved him from tumbling into the lower depths he saw on every side. For years he roamed the vastness of Russia, cadging his living in ways legal and illegal, appalled by the human depravity on every hand and attracted by the dangerous world of political activism.

Gorky's experiences "on the road" certainly pushed him toward his lifelong commitment to activism. His chaotic family life led him to do far better by his own dependents than had been done by him, although his arrangements were unorthodox. He had married Ekaterina Pavlovna in 1897; the following year they had a son, Maksim (sometimes also called Max in the letters that follow). Gorky had become conspicuous as an influential "liberal" writer and journalist in Czarist Russia. It became prudent for him to leave the country for longish periods. His success as a writer had made him financially comfortable, so he was able to travel as needed. Ekaterina Pavlovna stayed home, leading an active life herself. The two eventually separated, although they remained on close terms all of their lives and she visited him abroad.

In 1906 Gorky journeyed to America, where he caused great scandal not by preaching Bolshevism but by traveling with a woman, Maria Fedorovna Andreyeva, not his wife. Gorky left America with Maria Fedorovna, sailing to Naples, thence to Capri where he became the nucleus of a Russian émigré community. In Capri, Gorky's literary output included a volume of stories, *Tales from Italy*, which he himself declared dull and lifeless. His attentions, and all his energies, were always to be devoted to things Russian, and he never learned, or wanted to learn, either Italian or any other language.

When Gorky returned to Russia from Capri in 1913, he continued his prodigiously productive life of writing and political activism for several years, involving himself with yet another female companion, Maria Budberg. In the mare's nest of internal Russian intrigue, Gorky eventually found himself once more in an untenable position. Encouraged by his friend Lenin, he again sought exile abroad, the stated reason being his bad health (and indeed he suffered increasingly from a tubercular lung and other problems). Gorky lived in Sorrento fairly steadily from 1924 until 1931, then alternately in Sorrento and Russia until his permanent return to the USSR in 1933.

As a boy, Gorky's son Max lived first with his mother and then more and more with Gorky, especially during the days in southern Italy. When Max married in turn, he and his growing family lived with Gorky in Sorrento. Gorky's Sorrento letters, especially those to Ekaterina Pavlovna, reveal his love for his growing "tribe" of Peshkovs. He is as devoted to them as to his work, and revolutionary or not, as charmed as can be by his granddaughters. Gorky sometimes affectionately calls Ekaterina Pavlovna "mother" in his letters, and he teases her gently, scolding her for bad prose. She should know better, he jokes; after all, she's been closely associated with one of Russia's "loftiest" writers (Gorky was a tall man) for thirty years now.

From Letter 115. *To E. P. Peshkova*

17 January 1925

The weather here is wonderful; it's hot and everything is fine. Max is well, of course; the day before yesterday he [and some visitors] went over to Capri, spent the night there and returned yesterday, after having a good look round. Maksim said that "it felt like home" to him and he would apparently like to live there; but as he himself points out, there is a horde of Milanese innkeepers who are rapidly turning Capri into a resort, so that the local populace, the fishermen, have been driven to the point of contemplating a move to Calabria. It's true.

You are right: I don't listen to music here because I am tied to my desk. However, I'll finish my work in a few days and go to Naples for a vacation. There's a good opera in San Carlo, and I'll also go to the Symphony once or twice.

From Letter 118. *To E. P. Peshkova*

2 June 1925

It's a shame you can't come here now, mother, but it would be very good if you could come by September, for a month or six weeks. You must do this without fail, no matter what. A first birth is no joking matter: I well remember what it cost you. And Timosha has a nervous disposition. She's feeling good at the moment, even somewhat blissful, it seems, but I'm afraid that when the pregnancy becomes difficult, she will be scared. She's on very good terms with Mariia Ignatievna [Budberg], who is most knowledgeable about medicine, and she is also on good terms with me. But Max, in his egotism, is not sufficiently attentive towards her, and it would be good if you could write and tell him (only, please, without mentioning me!) that a pregnant wife, and not a bad one either, needs his affection and care. Do write. He nearly went off on a trip in his car to Sicily recently, but I managed to dissuade him. I would also have been worried if he had gone alone: gangsters are on the loose in Calabria, and the Fascists are not always so considerate in their treatment of foreigners either. He has no time for anything except his automobile at the moment: he goes off driving somewhere every day. Early this morning he took off for Naples. He's become much stronger and has put on weight, which everyone remarks upon.

...

I had never thought, mother, that I would live to attain the rank of grandfather, and I must admit that I'm enjoying it! It lifts the spirit. The Peshkovs are not a superfluous tribe; they've got talent, the devils! Oh, how richly endowed that damned Maksim is: he amazes artists with his talent even though he has never studied anywhere. But he doesn't want to do anything, no matter what you say! It's offensive. He's as egotistical as a pretty woman. All right, I'll stop.

...

... I have been immersed for a year or more in a novel, the largest book that I have ever written in terms of size. It is large in terms of its theme too. I sit here like a prisoner.

From Letter 130. *To E. P. Peshkova*

14 October 1926

It's most amusing to watch Marfa running about and to hear her squeals of joy as she says 'I can do it myself', which she accompanies with a theatrical laugh and a toss of her head. She's rather capricious and nervous, although the nurse is trying to cure her of her caprices, and not without success. She's an amusing little lass.

Maksim is well. He is buying a car, and often goes to Naples...

From Letter 142. *To E. P. Peshkova*

27 November 1927

Now that you have had medals pinned on you by bourgeois governments inimical to the Russian people, you have begun to write this kind of Russian: "drinks tea from the cup *which was dispatched by Maksim.*" Shame on you; you went to a gymnasium, and you have been personally acquainted for thirty years now with one of the loftiest Russian writers, a writer upon whom they have pinned every imaginable sin, and will continue to do so until the end of his days, and even beyond.

And another thing: you promised, you swore you would send me some books, but they haven't come. Shame on you again.

So please send:

Publisher: Zemlia i fabrika
Joseph Conrad, *Lord Jim.*
idem., Under Western Eyes

Be quick about it. By way of an advance, I'll tell you some stories about the girls. Dashka is a huge girl, she's already wearing the clothes that Marfa wore when she was six months old. Dashka has a calm disposition. When her mother finishes nursing her, she rumbles and belches. She smiles toothlessly at her grandfather and at the sun; the former finds this flattering, while the latter gets embarrassed and hides behind clouds. None the less Odarka remains a rather vague sort; that's probably because she is not yet two months old.

Marfa will probably be a lawyer and a café *chanteuse.* She is terribly talkative in three languages and her singing reveals that she has a good ear and also a penchant for a lively repertoire. She says, "Ganpa, les sang" and "Lo, ganpa." She calls her mother "Timosa." She's becoming clever and wilful. And less nervous. She scratches the pimples on her face, looks at herself in the mirror and grimaces. She likes listening to music more and more, but when she does so, she gets coy and embarrassed for some unknown reason. In general, she's an excellent woman.

...

There's no time for me to write, damn it!
Send the books!

Gorky's correspondents included dozens of well known figures inside Russia and out, ranging from writers like Boris Pasternak and George Bernard Shaw to major Soviet political figures like Lenin and Stalin. In this 1930 letter to Joseph Stalin, he offers a remarkable plea against the censorship unfortunately so typical of the Soviet regime.

Letter 154. *To I. V. Stalin*

8 January 1930

Dear Iosif Vissarionovich!

There is a report in *Rul'* that a certain journal in Chita has been punished for not having written in my praise. If one counts the Central Committee's reprimand to the people in Novosibirsk, this is the second such incident. I am quite sure that there will be a third, a tenth, etc. Although I consider this phenomenon both natural and inevitable, I do not think it is necessary to punish those who write about me in an uncomplimentary or hostile manner.

Like you, and all the other 'old-timers', I receive many hostile letters. The crazy ideas and attacks contained in these letters convince me that, ever since the Party set the countryside so decisively on the track of collectivization, the social revolution has begun to assume a truly socialist character. This is an upheaval of almost geological proportions, and it is greater, immeasurably greater and more profound, than anything that has yet been done by the Party. A way of life which has existed for thousands of years, an order which has created people of singular monstrosity, people quite horrifying in their animal conservatism and proprietorial instinct – this order is being destroyed. There are some 20 million such people. The problem of re-educating them in the shortest possible time is an insanely difficult one. Yet it is being resolved in a practical way right now.

It is quite natural that many of these millions are falling prey to a truly violent insanity. They don't even understand the full depth of the upheaval which is taking place, yet they sense instinctively, in their bones, that the very deepest foundations of their antiquated life are beginning to be destroyed. A ruined church can be rebuilt and you can install any God you like in it, but when the ground slips away beneath your feet – that is irreparable and for all time. So now we find people cursing furiously. These are people who have mechanically acquired revolutionary phrases and a revolutionary lexicon, yet who very often conceal beneath such phrases the vindictive mood of an ancient person for whom 'the end is nigh'. Note that these curses are strongest of all in Siberia and the Far East, and that is where the peasant is strongest too.

But "names will never hurt me"; they will never keep me from living. As for my work, such abuse serves only as a stimulus. As you know, I am not a Party member, which means that nothing addressed to me can touch the Party or its leaders. So let them curse. All the more so since some people – indeed, many people – curse out of ignorance and a lack of understanding, so that when you explain the crux of the matter to them, they stop. Many people hasten to declare their orthodoxy, thereby hoping to gain something for themselves, and they do gain certain things.

Generally speaking, however, everything is going very well – much better than could have been expected. And so, I beg of you, please do not punish those who curse. Some of them are incurable and not worth thinking about, whereas others are only slightly ill and they will get better. Our life itself is a most skilful doctor.

Let me take this opportunity to congratulate you once again on your fifty years of service to life. Fine service it has been too.

Keep well!

A. Peshkov

Will you write something for *Literaturnaia ucheba*? You should. It would be very useful for beginning writers. Very. Do write something!

A. P.

Isaac Babel

Among the Russian visitors to Maksim Gorky's "apartment" villa in Sorrento was the writer Isaac Babel, whose short stories are among literature's best. Always generous with his support, Gorky had encouraged the younger writer in his craft and was among the first to publish his writings. When Babel came to Sorrento in 1933, he found Gorky typically hospitable. Babel's letters reveal how much he, too, wants the companionship of family around him, even in paradise – he is doing all he can to arrange for his wife Zhenya and daughter Natasha to join him.

In letters to his mother and sister, Babel writes about life in Sorrento. He had little of Gorky's prolixity – it was hard for him to generate material, and an official Soviet writers' group leaned on him for what it considered Babel's suspicious silence. Soviet writers were supposed to write in support of the state, well and often. As early as 1925, Gorky had noted that Babel was courting trouble – probably he had in mind literary trouble – by being so terse. Writing in May 1925 to M. L. Slonimsky, Gorky noted that Babel "is also a major talent; he is most cunning and shrewd in the way he deals with his experiences, he does not spare his 'imagination' and has the ability to be almost epic." But, Gorky added, "his brevity has a double-edged quality: it could either prove instructive to him or else be his undoing."

As it turned out, when Babel returned to Russia in 1933, he did get into trouble, increasingly serious political trouble – investigations, questionings, detention, because of his failure to produce on demand. When Babel was arrested in 1939, he disappeared from sight and no one knows exactly what happened. Documents that came to light later, maybe fraudulent ones, give the date of his death as 1941.

Babel's letters from paradise are characteristically terse. Gorky figures prominently in them. It would seem, from Babel's observations, that by 1933 Gorky was living far more exuberantly than he let on in his 1931 letter to Popov. In the excerpts below from letters to his mother and sister, Babel gives an attractive description of an unlikely pair of revolutionaries in paradise.

ISAAC BABEL, selected letters from Nathalie Babel, *Isaac Babel: The Lonely Years 1925-1939* (1964)

Naples, April 13, 1933

It appears that everything they write in the geography books is true. There are places here of glorious, unlikely beauty. I'm not really myself again yet. We'll sort ourselves out bit by bit and then I'll write in more detail.

My address: Poste Restante, Sorrento, Italy.
I'm waiting impatiently for news from you.

Sorrento, April 15, 1933

The earthly paradise, I suppose, must look about like the Capo di Sorrento. The emerald sea is spread out before the window, olive, orange and lemon groves grow right up to the door. It's only now that I'm recovering my senses after so much blissful beauty. I must work so that I can quickly drag my ladies over here. Our grand old man [Gorky] is well, cheerful and unwearied. He's planning to go to Moscow in the middle of May...

Sorrento, April 18, 1933

They've found me a room "out of the way," here. It has a terrace looking out over the Bay of Naples. The weather is really magical. The lights of Naples, Castellamare, Vesuvius. An uncanny beauty. Gorky is leaving some time in the second half of May and has invited me and my family to stay in his house. It's tempting and very convenient. As there's an incredible mess here, I don't want Zhenya to come with Natasha before the beginning of May. I wrote to her to that effect today. I've already started work and little by little am getting into my stride. Working conditions here are such as I've never had in my whole life.

Sorrento, April 24, 1933

Have received a letter from you at last... We've been having bad weather here all the time, but today it looks as if it might improve. I am working with pleasure here under such conditions – quiet, solitude, peace – as I have never had in my life before. I miss Natasha very much. Financial matters are holding them up. I'm hoping they'll get here at the beginning of May. In a few days I shall read a "story" I have written to Gorky and his advice will determine all my future plans.

He and I have been to Capri and today we're going to look around Naples. He knows every stone here. There are two more excursions I have to make – to Vesuvius and to Herculaneum and Pompei (all these places are very close by) but I want to wait for Zhenya and we'll go together...

Sorrento, May 2, 1933

The sirocco, a suffocating tropical wind, is blowing. It's a grand picture – "trees bending low," the sea wrapped in an oppressive, milky fog.

...

I've completed a Herculean task – a play. As, of course, it does not fit in with the "general Party line," it can expect rough going, but everyone wholeheartedly acknowledges its artistic qualities.* The setting and the

---

* Babel was finishing the play *Maria,* which was ultimately published in the March, 1935, issue of *Teatr i dramaturgiya* [*Theater and Drama*]. What he foresees here was fully confirmed; the drama aroused a great dispute and was eventually banned. [Nathalie Babel's note.]

characters are new ones, such as I've never used before, and if it comes off I shall be happy. In a few days, when I start typing it, I'll ask for advice.

Yesterday, I spent the whole day in Naples with Gorky. He took us to the museums, showed us ancient sculpture (I'm still breathless with admiration), paintings by Titian, Raphael and Velasquez. We had lunch and dinner together. The old man drank, and he drank plenty. In the evening, we went to a restaurant located on a hill above the town (a fairy-tale view from there). Everyone in the establishment has known him for thirty years and they all got up when he came in. The waiters rushed to kiss his hands [sic] and immediately sent for the old-timers who sing Neapolitan songs. They came running – seventy-year-olds who remembered Gorky well – and they sang in their cracked old voices in a way I will never forget. Gorky wept unrestrainedly, drank constantly and when they tried to take his glass away from him, kept saying: "It's the last time in my life." For me, it was an unforgettable day.

I am trying hard to speed Zhenya's and Natasha's coming. I hope that they will arrive in ten days or so.

I have been advised to send my play by mail. Of course, I really ought to take it myself. I haven't decided yet what I will do. The Gorkys are leaving on the ninth – there's a Soviet ship going from London to Odessa and it is, of course, most convenient for them to take it. Besides me, there'll be only Marshak, our superb children's poet, in the house, and I hope he will take to Natasha. Marshak also has a sister in Brussels and possibly we will all go to Belgium together.

Gorky has taken three of my new stories for his almanac. I am really quite pleased with one of them – I only hope the censors will pass it. Gorky has promised to send me my fees in foreign currency.

Sorrento, May 11, 1933

The Gorkys left on the 8th. They took a train to Genoa where they caught the Soviet boat that will take them straight to Odessa. I saw my "master" off as far as Naples, stayed there a couple of days, then came back here yesterday evening. Now, I am alone with Marshak in the huge stone villa and wish Zhenya and Natasha would come very soon. They are, of course, held up by financial difficulties that I hope we shall be able to overcome.

CHAPTER 8

THE TWILIGHT OF THE SUPERMEN
NIETZSCHE AND THE WAGNERS IN SORRENTO

In the autumn of 1876, Richard and Cosima Wagner and their long-time friend Friedrich Nietzsche ran into each other in Sorrento. The meeting between "The Master" and his devoted disciple was not planned but the repercussions were great. It precipitated what was soon to become a permanent break between the two.

Decades later, Adolf Hitler came to regard both Friedrich Nietzsche (1844-1900) and Richard Wagner (1813-1883) as early formulators of his "Aryan" vision. Today we tend to think of them as having similar ideas. Great men, yes, but unpleasantly tainted by the dangerous cult of the Aryan Superman, for which, as it were, Nietzsche wrote the lyrics and Wagner the music. The works of these two men can plausibly be seen as forming part of the foundation on which Nazism and the Holocaust were built.

During the Sorrento interlude, which is a landmark event in the relationship between the two, Nietzsche and Wagner grew somehow disaffected with each other. They were never to meet again. Within a year the breach between them had become open and permanent.

In happier times, Nietzsche had been a mainstay in the circle around Wagner, even staying in the household at Tribschen (Switzerland). It was, to say the least, an unusual household. Cosima Lizst (1837-1930, illegitimate daughter of the famous pianist and composer) was its center. Wagner also lived in the house, although Cosima was still officially married to Baron von Bülow – a complication that required Wagner to insist to his patron, King Ludwig, that his relationship with Cosima was innocent and that she was his "secretary." The family was initially rounded out by the four daughters Cosima had had by both men. During one of Nietzsche's early visits, Cosima gave birth to Siegfried, her last child and Wagner's only son. Since Cosima was still married to von Bülow at the time, she and Wagner were faced with the problem of how to legitimate Siegfried as Richard's child. Eventually Cosima was able to divorce von Bülow and marry Richard.

Nietzsche's status as a brilliant young professor, as well as the power of his pen to promote the cause of Wagner's art, made the philosopher a useful adjunct to the camp of the Wagnerites. Nietzsche for his part was drawn to the magnetic, dominant Wagner (and his equally powerful wife) no less than to the music and its ideas.

Exactly what happened at Sorrento no one can say. The letters don't reveal anything. Nor does Cosima's diary, which provides the most complete record of the period. The most widely accepted explanation is that Nietzsche drew the line at Wagner's ostentatious new-found Christianity, seeing it as a betrayal of higher ideals. Nietzsche's sister believes the break was inevitable: Nietzsche simply outgrew Wagner. Nietzsche had participated in the Bayreuth Festival in 1876, at some cost to his health, and was sorely disenchanted by its bombast and vulgarity.

Still other commentators argue that Nietzsche might have broken with Wagner over the latter's antisemitism, which was particularly offensive in Sorrento because it was not just theoretical but directed against Nietzsche's Jewish traveling companion, and perhaps lover, Paul Rée. Another related possibility: the cause of the rupture between Wagner and Nietzsche might have been Nietzsche's homosexuality, if indeed he was homosexual; opinions differ. Nietzsche's sexuality is such a mystery to his biographers that at least one of them maintains that the philosopher had no sexual life whatsoever but contracted syphilis (which certainly lay behind a lot of his physical problems) in a non-sexual way: through attending to the wounds of an infected soldier during a brief stint as a medical orderly.

It's also possible that Nietzsche's fascination with Cosima Wagner began to eclipse that with Richard, so that the philosopher came to think of the composer as an interloper in what ought to have been a union of destiny between Cosima and himself. One of Nietzsche's final acts before his institutionalization was to write to Cosima (Wagner was dead by then) claiming her as his wife. Cosima never replied.

Here are passages from Cosima's journal from the time of the Wagners' arrival in Sorrento, October 5, 1876, through November 6, 1876, which encompasses the period when the Wagners and Nietzsche were all three in residence there. Nietzsche got to Sorrento around October 27; it seems the Wagners were not aware that he would be arriving. In her journal, Cosima shows herself a careful observer of the life around her. But Nietzsche's visit seems almost to have escaped her attention; it would be very easy to overlook the two occasions she notes meeting with him (October 27 and November 2). According to other accounts, the two households had met far more often for walks, conversations, and excursions, but these events are not recorded anywhere by the principals.

As his reprinted letter shows, Wagner was clearly preoccupied with the financial disaster of the first Bayreuth Festival just a few months earlier; he is unable to focus on much else. The letter is typical of the handful he wrote from Sorrento, with its worries about finances and feeling unappreciated. Nietzsche wrote almost fifty letters during the period of his stay, but they are no more informative than the reprinted one about his relationship with Wagner. Nietzsche was already a semi-invalid by this time, suffering from horrible headaches and painful problems with his eyes – he could write little. A few phrases from his letter of October 28, 1876, to his sister are vaguely attentive to his surroundings; other letters from the period speak of his maladies.

These surviving Sorrentine documents reveal little of the seething psychosexual currents swirling around the three protagonists, and give scarcely a hint that a previously fervent friendship had existed or was drawing to a close. Taken together, they are a useful reminder that some things will always remain a mystery.

COSIMA WAGNER, *Diaries 1869-1877* (1978)

Thursday, October 5 [1876] Departure for Sorrento [from Naples]; as the ship leaves, beggars swim around in the water, among them a boy who stands out on account of his brown skin, his beauty and liveliness and agility – "like something direct from Nature's workshop," says R. – he gathers the coins thrown into the sea in his mouth. On the ship singers and guitarists and fiddlers, cheerful and mournful popular songs, at the same time wickerwork and oysters being bartered, all languages being spoken; while a dark-blue sea sings its eternal lullaby, and the blue line of hills encloses it all – a curious dream! Is it its strangeness or its familiarity which makes us feel so melancholy – a gentle yearning, I might call it, but for what? not for living! – A gentleman from Magdeburg speaks to R., he was at our performances and speaks very nicely about them. Sorrento, the Hôtel Vittoria, we have taken the little cottage beside the hotel, wonderful peace – During the siesta hours R. and I read, to ourselves, Sismondi's *Les Républiques d'Italie.*

Friday, October 6 [1876] Picked up lessons with the children again; they have forgotten quite a bit! In the afternoon a very lovely donkey ride to the Deserto, R. and I admit to each other that all our delight lies in the delight of the children; up above, a good Franciscan, splendid terrace, but in the little church two pupils playing dance music of the most wretched kind. Merry ride home, my donkey called Fantasia! The driver promises it *macaron tutto formaggio* to liven it up. [*In the margin:* "Walk to the ravines."]...

Saturday, October 7 [1876] Still lovely weather, work with the children, sea baths, reading Sismondi, and – alas! – many, many worried thoughts. The ride to the Deserto, entered for yesterday by mistake...

Monday, October 9 [1876] At 8 o'clock set sail for Capri, breakfast in the Hôtel du Louvre, whose ridiculous name amuses us greatly; ride to the Villa Tiberio; stop at the Leap; our donkey girls dance the tarantella for us; the eldest of them with great passion, but one of them is not permitted to dance, says her husband is jealous. Our ride home through narrow lanes resembles an Arab wedding procession, everything splendid! The poverty of the people in comparison with the richness of Nature astonishes one; but this poverty would not exist – or at least the mania for profit – if there were not strangers here to beg from. I felt shame, too, in making them dance the tarantella. Journey home amid shooting stars and phosphorescent waves! Unforgettable impression; the white houses in all that green, the splendid flowers, later the calm sea, a perfect summer night. Unfortunately, however, the shadow of gloomy thoughts at home. R. is wondering whether he should repeat the performances! Not a single one of the princes, having distributed decorations to all the participants, has asked R. what can be done for him, how he might be helped or supported!...

Tuesday, October 10 [1876] 23 years ago I saw R. for the first time, being led by my father, coming to see us children; practically all those then with me are now gone!... Give lessons to the children while R. is writing his address to the patrons. Spent the afternoon on the splendid terrace, from which one looks out over an olive grove and the sea. In the evening wrote to my father...

Wednesday, October 11 [1876] Lessons, bathing, reading, a resumption of our Tribschen life, unfortunately with many reflections for and against; for R., how to get the performances started again?...

Thursday, October 12 [1876] R. not well; perhaps the soft air does not agree with him? He is not sleeping well. – Lulu's birthday today, we drink to her. – Spent the afternoon sitting on the little terrace, on one side the olive grove, on the other the sea. We read Sismondi together with great enjoyment...

Friday, October 13 [1876] R. begins a sort of spa cure (*eau de Vichy*), and the pretty morning walks seem to do him good. He writes to Herr von Schl., telling him something of his situation and saying that the only thing at the festival which was really successful was what the Schleinitzes themselves brought about! Walk in the afternoon – in the evening the tarantella danced by Sorrento people in the hall of the hotel; also some of their plays. One of the women extremely graceful in an unstudied, natural sort of way. At the end *"Die Wacht am Rhein"*! Our waiter confessed to us that he had been in Berlin and had brought it back and taught it to the people here!

Saturday, October 14 [1876] Fidi slightly unwell. Lessons for the children. R. writes to Herr v. Radowitz, asking him for his opinion about what should be done. I give the children lessons; in the afternoon a walk; this spot is becoming increasingly dear to me; the paths between two walls with overhanging trees, the ravines and rocks, the olive trees, it has all become so familiar to me, and I also hear nothing upsetting here. Only R.'s worries can hardly be banished, even for a few moments, and so the horizon is clouded.

Sunday, October 15 [1876] A free day for the children, for me a day of writing letters and reading (Sismondi and Nietzsche's paper again). Sirocco.

Monday, October 16 [1876] Moving; we leave the pretty cottage, which is slightly damp, and move to the 3rd floor of the big hotel. I am always rather reluctant to change rooms, it makes me feel melancholy.

Tuesday, October 17 [1876] Lessons for the children, resumption of music lessons. Sirocco, the sea rough. R. still somewhat worn out, but in cheerful spirits. Talked a lot about Goethe; *Faust* much more valuable than the *Divina Commedia*, but less variability in it...

Wednesday, October 18 [1876] The boat which carries the mail from Sorrento to Capri capsized yesterday, seven people were saved, but one was drowned. Such things are reported, and heard with indifference here, and how indifferent, too, the whole outside world, romping in the sun again today!... Wrote on R.'s behalf to the secretary of the Royal Academy in Stockholm, with thanks for his nomination. R. starts a long letter to the King, once again describing the whole situation to him and suggesting that he take over the whole thing [i.e., financing the Bayreuth festival]. Watched the sunset with R. from the terrace; thoughts of Odysseus swimming. I already feel quite at home in this country. In the evening read with R. the touching story of Pope Celestine V. – Frequent thoughts of giving up the festival entirely and disappearing – but would that be good for the children?

Thursday, October 19 [1876] At 5 o'clock toiling of the canonical hour, an ugly jangle indeed, our German bells speak with a different voice! – R. not well, has to go to bed, where he remains for part of the day. I give the children their lessons, read the life of Dante, two cantos of the *Purgatorio* and parts of the *Républiques italiennes*.

Friday, October 20 [1876] R. still unwell, which throws me into a truly melancholy mood. My own salvation, work with the children; bathing in the sea very strange, for the waves very powerful. In the afternoon R. gets up, he is somewhat better, but still very weak; the weather clears up, I take out a boat and float for a while on the sea, constantly changing, in eternal motion, neither wave nor cloud pays heed to my woe, and the motionless mountain throws it back; movement and rigidity, deaf and unreceptive; will a mortal being hear the sound? Perhaps a mother's heart! – We talk to R. about the beauty of this spot. "Yes," he observes, "if one did not always bring one's thoughts with one."

Saturday, October 21 [1876] Stormy night, hail, thunder, and I don't know what else. R. dreamed of my execution: I had come to an agreement with my father that, in order to atone for my marriage to R., I must be executed, only Lulu should accompany me; he had not believed it at first, but when he saw me being carried off on a bier (because I could not walk), he had cried out, and his cry woke him up. Before that he had dreamed that *Siegfried* was being performed and something went wrong on the stage. "Brandt, the lights are going out!" – With these words he woke up! – Lessons for the children, R. finishes his letter to the King, to whom he makes the proposal either to recommend our festival to the Reich through a representative or to take the whole thing over himself. – Read Sismondi. Spent much time reflecting in the evening, firm resolve to fight against melancholy, which is threatening to drive me mad.

Sunday, October 22 [1876] " 'Tis a consummation devoutly to be wish'd" – these words come into my mind as I think of my father's birthday and wonder how he must look back on his life! – Today is a letter day for me (11!), R. writes to Frau Lucca, apologizing for not being able to give her the cuts she requested for *Rienzi* in Bologna. In the afternoon a lovely walk to Capo di Sorrento – a terrible thunderstorm during the night has cleared the sky and refreshed the earth. The walk does R. good, we let ourselves go in one of those endless conversations which have always taken place between us; this time about the Normans, fascinating in their influence in the South, unsympathetic in the North against the Saxons.

Monday, October 23 [1876] R. complains of a restless night, but he decides to keep to the outing to Pompeii with the bevy of children. It is very successful, and, if R. and I are somewhat tired, we nevertheless return home in a very cheerful mood. In the evening I glance through some books (sent to us to look at); everything about the festival absurd, and particularly about R. – Quite apart from all this activity, R. feels, there must certainly be people who were deeply moved by the performances.

Tuesday, October 24 [1876] R. had a good night and at the breakfast table tells us a lot about his childhood years: Eisleben, Possendorf, his cousin Fredi, giving free lessons, etc. Then lessons for the children on my part, while R. has to write a reply to the Berlin horn player; the King bestowed medals on three players (the concertmaster Grützmacher, the oboist Wieprecht, and Fleischhauer) – these do not write to thank R., but all the others attack him! – Visit from Malwida, who is looking for an apartment for friend Nietzsche and inspects several houses. She returns to Naples in the evening. Conversation with R.

Wednesday, October 25 [1876] R. well as a result of a good night. Cheerful breakfast, then lessons for the children and bathing for me, R. reads through his preface for Villot, since he is preparing a reply to Herr Monod's letter. He also reads the *Républiques italiennes*, with great sympathy for the town of Pisa and the hero Castruccione. – Lovely walk in the afternoon with the children and R., we wander for two hours along the water's edge, where I already feel entirely at home. Return home in a thunderstorm. In the evening glanced again through several books forwarded to us; the recognition of R.'s achievement insignificant, the rest incredibly silly and perfidious. A Herr Schletterer writes in the Augsburg paper, literally inciting the orchestra players not to enter the orchestra pit and to abandon R. to his own devices! These people stir up all the base human instincts – that is the extent of their wisdom, which so lamentably abandons them as soon as they enter the world of ideas! – Another little booklet by a Herr Dunkl, designed virtually as a glorification of my father, throws out in passing the remark that my brother, Daniel, was not at all gifted!

Thursday, October 26 [1876] Work with the children while the olive harvest is going on, with its attendant yodeling; the people here just warble like birds. – Yesterday R. woke me up with a lovely improvisation; I should like to persuade him to forget all the *Nibelungen* troubles and to start on a new work. He was thinking again recently about a symphony of mourning for those who fell in the war, in which he would use his *Romeo and Juliet* theme. He saw the coffins being brought into a hall, more and more of them, so that individual grief was gradually submerged in general suffering. Only after that the song of triumph. But who shares his feelings? A wonderful drive in the afternoon, visited all the grottoes between Meta and Sorrento, thinking of Dante and Doré; splendid sky, the island lying blissfully before us in a golden light, Vesuvius with the villages on its slopes, reddish-gray and brownish-gold, somberly threatening. From Meta, home on foot, a long walk in the moonlight; everything looking wonderful, the houses as much as the gardens with their tall stone-pines, those aristocrats among trees. In the evening we are indeed somewhat tired, but in splendid spirits. I feel as if life has granted me a respite here!

Friday, October 27 [1876] Talked about Barbarossa and Arnold of Brescia, the great sin of the former in delivering him up, an act avenged on his whole family line – *Der Ring des Nibelungen*, Wotan's sin. – I tell R. that I cannot understand why our modern writers do not treat these subjects, which so closely affect us, instead of going in search of Nero and God knows what else. – Nice day, bathing with the children. In the afternoon took a little walk with R. and the children, then sat for a long time with R. on our terrace and looked at the sea. After that a visit from Malwida, Dr. Rée, and our friend Nietzsche, the latter very run down and much concerned with his health. They are staying in Sorrento. – In the evening R. reads me the fine, detailed letter which he has written to Herr Monod in reply to his enthusiastic missive; in it he discusses his attitude toward the French. – Moonlight over the olive garden, thought of Christ: "If it be possible, let this cup pass from me; nevertheless not as I will, but as thou wilt" – the epitome of all suffering and all salvation; how often does the soul beseech that the cup may pass, how hard to submit, and how seldom does it succeed in doing so! But when it does succeed, how the wings spread, how the soul is borne up to the purest heights, beyond the reach of everything!

Saturday, October 28 [1876] Lessons for the children, seeing Malwida, whose birthday it is today. Read much Sismondi, always with great interest.

Sunday, October 29 [1876] Day for games and letters; also bathing and Sismondi. I beg R. to work on the biography, but he feels no great urge, he cannot get his "*Qualhall*" [*word play on "Valhalla," "Qual" meaning "torture"*] out of his mind.

Monday, October 30 [1876] Visit to Malwida with the children, in splendid weather. R. constantly reading Sismondi, with much enjoyment. We go for a walk in the afternoon. He is, as he tells me, grateful for everything which distracts him from the round of thoughts so oppressing him. We admit to each other that we frequently keep silent just in order not to have to impart to each other our gloomy thoughts concerning the present situation and all our past experiences. In the evening read some of Herr v. Hagen's writings. – R. has been looking through San-Marte's *Parzival* in a search for names, but he says it is very abstruse and of no use at all. Telegram from Judith [Mendès-Gautier], saying, "Tremendous success of Siegfried's 'Funeral March' at Pasdeloup's, with fights and two duels." Herr Unger also writes, a reminder of distasteful things!

Tuesday, October 31 [1876] R. reads, and writes to Councilor Düfflipp about a decoration for the architect Brückwald, who has been unjustly ignored, while Herr Brandt has been overwhelmed with decorations. – We celebrate Malwida's birthday today with an outing on donkeys to the Deserto, to the jubilation of the children. The vegetation has lost a lot since our first visit, but it is still lovely, and Heaven sends us a very fine sunset as a parting gift. In the evening read, with R., Sismondi's comparison between Greece and Italy, then conversed.

Wednesday, November [1876] All Saints' Day. Very bad weather, so that R. says he believes it is rather All Fiends' Day which had been loosed upon us. In the evening we are visited by Dr. Rée, whose cold and precise character does not appeal to us; on closer inspection we come to the conclusion that he must be an Israelite.

Thursday, November 2 [1876] All Souls' Day, the weather fine again, we take a nice walk, and the evening we spend with our friends Malwida and Prof. Nietzsche.

Friday, November 3 [1876] Letter from my father, also from Herr v. Schleinitz, very friendly, but nothing from Herr v. Radowitz; only friend Heckel writes and says that it is not R.'s task to approach the patrons about paying off the deficit, that the patrons themselves should take this over, settle it among themselves. He is the only one so far to show any feeling in the matter. Otherwise all we perceive is scorn and sneering. A newspaper reports that Richter received four decorations in Bayreuth, all earned with "sour sweat." Then in the Augsburg paper a travel article about Todi, in which the reporter suddenly, without any reason, introduces the Bayreuth festival, attributing R.'s great power to Mormonism – in short, the most vexatious things one can imagine. R. deeply upset, I beseech him to take no notice of all these things and to answer them with silence.

Saturday, November 4 [1876] Bathing still for me and the children, both today and yesterday; we are preparing for our departure for Rome. R. assiduously reads Sismondi in order not to think about the things that grieve him. Heckel has suggested a fourth performance to cover the deficit. We discuss the necessity of charging for seats, which would compromise everything from the very start, then the angry mood of the singers when they are not allowed to appear again at the end. R. says the job ought to be done by people who take pleasure in such things, very well, it should be a sect; but can such people be found? Not in sufficient numbers when curiosity is lacking. Much worry, bitter worry. Our only comfort the children.

Sunday, November 5 [1876] Winter has come; the sea is driving along its white horses and the wind blows cold; we think of leaving. Malwida has lunch with us, we attempt an outing, but the wind drives us homeward. I write several letters. R. reads Sismondi, the children play, go for another swim and take a long walk to Massa. We witness celebrations in the hotel and on the square over the election of a deputy! In the evening, conversation with R., during which I try to talk about all sorts of strange things, but we always come back to the one dismal subject. R. says that his main feeling during the performances was, "Never again, never again!" He winced so much, he says, that the King asked him what was the matter, and then he had to restrain himself forcibly.

Monday, November 6 [1876] Decision to leave this beautiful place tomorrow...

RICHARD WAGNER, *Letters* (1927)

Sorrento, 7th October, 1876

... I am thinking of asking for my friends' advice as to whether I should apply to the Emperor to cover any deficit. A single bold attack would make it clear whether my labours are to be rewarded merely by the distribution of Orders to the participants or whether they are to be directly recognized in the only way I could acknowledge *as* recognition, namely, by the covering of expenses, which most certainly ought not to become a burden upon *me*. Also, this might perhaps pave the way towards bringing my petition for future support for the Bayreuth Dramatic Festival before the imperial Council as an Imperial Government measure. Fortunately, it only needs a certain amount of time to clear this matter up, and time we still have, as the business has not to be finally settled till November.

I received a very fine letter from the King in Venice. He exhorts me to patience and perseverance, and he will put my affairs before everything else.

Consequently, I hope to see everything wound up before the end of this year, and at the New Year to be able to begin preparing for a repetition of the Festival. This last costs me great self-denial for, particularly if I get the necessary recognition and support, I shall feel bound to take a very strenuous and active part in correcting the performances of my personnel, and I have little spirit or inclination for that at present. –

FRIEDRICH NIETZSCHE, *Briefe 1875-1879* (1980), trans. by Linnea Vacca 1999

Sorrento, 28 October 1876

Here we are, in Sorrento. The whole trip from Bex to here took 8 days. In Genoa I was sick. From there it took about three days by sea, and, you know, we escaped seasickness. I prefer this kind of travel to going by train, which I hate. We met Fraulein von Meysenbug in a hotel in Naples and traveled together with her yesterday to our new home, Villa Rubinacci, Sorrento by Naples. I have an entire huge high room, fronting onto a terrace. I've just come back from my first swim; the water was warmer, according to Rée, than the North Sea in July. Yesterday evening we were at the Wagners, which is five minutes from us, they live in the Hotel Victoria and will be staying here the month of November.

Sorrento and Naples are beautiful – people don't exaggerate it. The air here is a mix of mountain and sea. It's very good for my eyes. Under my terrace extends a large wooded garden (which remains green even in the winter), and beyond that the very dark sea, and yet beyond, Vesuvius.

Let us hope...

Nietzsche's letter ends on a hopeful note, but little else did. The Wagners left Sorrento not long after Nietzsche's arrival, earlier than had been foreseen by Nietzsche. The gulf between them, whatever its cause, deepened and became permanent. Richard Wagner faced ongoing woes over Bayreuth. He continued to chafe over a perceived lack of recognition for his music (now, of course, he is acknowledged to be one of opera's handful of truly great composers). By 1883 Wagner was dead. Nietzsche's health continued to deteriorate, and although he outlived Wagner by almost two decades, he was neither well nor sane for the last years of his life. Only Cosima persevered, and she kept her journal for many years. It makes interesting reading, even if it seems to leave out some of the things readers would really like to know.

CHAPTER 9

"THIS IS BUT EARTH AFTER ALL"

When I went out on our loggia this morning, the sun was up, but still hidden behind the high eastern mountains. The fresh morning breeze gave exquisite purity to sea and sky; rosy and golden tints appeared through the mists that half veiled Ischia; a white edge, as of foam, softened the blue of the sea; the whole coast had a delicate grace of outlines, of hills melting on mountains, and mountains fading away on the morning paleness of the sky, that almost gave me a sense of sorrow, for it spoke of paradise, and this is but earth after all.

JULIA KAVANAGH

Even in paradise, there is discontent. Visitors who came seeking the sun, look out on rain or find the sun oppressive. They are overwhelmed by the supplications of beggars. The natives seem simple or distant. There is a feeling of repression. Nature is being destroyed...

On the Weather

HERBERT M. VAUGHAN, *The Naples Riviera* (1925)

It has been said of more than one spot on this globe, that it was so beautiful in summer the marvel was to think any one could die there; and so wretched in winter, it was a miracle for its inhabitants to survive. Sorrento may be said to belong to this class of place, for the climate of its short winter is one of the most trying and inclement that can possibly be imagined, whilst during spring, summer and early autumn it well merits its local reputation as *il piccolo paradiso* of the Bay of Naples, and its air is considered by Neapolitans as the "balm in Gilead" for every evil to which human flesh is heir. The Lactarian Mountains protect the plain of Sorrento in summer from the scorching rays of the sun, and lay their beneficent shadow for several hours of the long hot summer's day over the many thousands who dwell on the fertile Piano di Sorrento at their base. But in winter these same hills intercept the blessed sunshine, which is what most travellers speed southwards to obtain, and leave the coast line from Castellamare to the Punta di Sorrento with its northern aspect wrapped in shade and moisture, whilst the remainder of the Bay is still basking in the genial warmth, so that anything more miserable than a mid-winter sojourn in Sorrento it would be impossible to conceive. There are of course calm warm days to be met with even in December and January, but these are occasional and by no means dependable blessings, and the visitor who persists in taking up his abode here at this season of the year must prepare himself to experience cold, damp, wind and rain, without any of the contrivances or comforts of a northern winter. "One swallow does not make a summer," and on the same principle a southern latitude and the presence of orange groves do not necessarily imply a salubrious climate; indeed, the sub-tropical surroundings seem to add an extra degree of chilliness to the place. To sit at Christmastide in a large lofty room before a meagre fire of sputtering smoky logs, with Vesuvius wrapped from crest to base in a white mantle of new fallen snow, and with an icy *tramontana* from the bleak Abruzzi howling round the house, bending the bay trees and penetrating into every corner of the chamber, is by no means the ideal picture of a winter in the Sunny South; yet this is only what the traveller must be prepared to face, and is very likely to obtain...

HENRIK IBSEN, *The Correspondence* (1970)

August, 1881

... My wife suffers more than we do from the heat, and especially from the sirocco; but she manages to keep in health by bathing every day. I do not believe that you could have stood a whole summer down here. Walking is almost out of the question; one had to keep as still as possible.

AUGUSTUS J. C. HARE, *Cities of Southern Italy and Sicily* (1891)

Sorrento is delightfully cool in summer compared with other places in this part of Italy...

But the village looks north, and is often very damp and cold in winter; and in spring it is well to be prepared for the sudden change from the heat of Naples to the chill breezes here.

On Taking Walks

HERBERT M. VAUGHAN, *The Naples Riviera* (1925)

... Nor is the cold compensated for by any advantages in the neighbor-hood itself, for there is but the high road from Castellamare which passes through the town and leads above the seashore to Massa Lubrense. It is all very well in its way, but in wet weather its surface is one sheet of slippery mud, and the streams pouring down the hillside make it chilly and damp for all who are not quick walkers. Besides this not very attractive and soon exploited walk, there are only the *vicoletti*, the narrow steep rocky paths running up hill, which make rough going and give little pleasure, for they are almost all bounded on either side by high stone walls that jealously exclude the view...

W. J. A. STAMER, *Dolce Napoli* (1878)

... The second objection to Sorrento as a summer residence is the ab-sence of pleasant walks and drives... To enjoy it in summer, one must either have great resources in oneself or be a Turk and confirmed lotus-eater. If the visitor be neither artist, musician, scribbler, nor book-worm, all he can do is to gaze on the Gulf, dream away the long summer days in *loggia,* or orange-garden, and make *kief à la Moslem.* Life at Sorrento is what the French call *"la vie contemplative"*; and that style of existence does not suit the energetic Anglo-Saxon temperament.

AUGUSTUS J. C. HARE, *Cities of Southern Italy and Sicily* (1891)

In general, however, Sorrento is less agreeable for walking and riding than La Cava and Amalfi, as nearly all of the paths are shut in by high walls, obscuring the view, for a great distance from the town...

On Beggars

JAMES FENIMORE COOPER, *Excursions in Italy* (1838)

The great number of beggars that torment one like gnats was at first a drawback on our pleasures. It was no unusual thing to have a dozen of them in chase; and, if unprovided with change, we were often harassed by them until we returned to our own gate: for the poor Neapolitans, unlike the beggars of Paris, are not often provided with change. We have got relieved from them, however, by mere accident; and as the incident is characteristic, it is worth mentioning.

Walking one day on the terrace that overhangs the bay, I happened to cast my eyes over the balustrade into the street, where there is a public seat that is much frequented by idlers, immediately beneath our *drawing-room* window. It was occupied at the moment by an old fellow with a lame leg, as fine an old mendicant as one shall see in a thousand. This man was enjoying himself, and keeping an eye on the gate, in expectation of our daily sortie; for we had been a little irregular of late, and had given our tormentors the slip. Seeing me, the beggar rose and pulled off his cap. As I had no change, I called a servant to bring me a *grano*. This little ceremony established a sort of intercourse between us. The next day, the thing was repeated. As I usually wrote in the cabinet of a morning, and walked on the terrace at stated hours, my new acquaintance became very punctual; and there is such a pleasure in thinking you are making a fellow-creature comfortable for a day at so cheap a rate, that I began to expect him. This lasted ten days, perhaps, when I found *two,* one fine morning, instead of the *one* I had known. The other *grano* was given, and the next day I had *three* pensioners. These three swelled like the men in buckram, and were soon a dozen. From that moment no one asked charity of us in our walks: we frequently met beggars, but they invariably drew modestly aside, permitting us to pass without question. We might have been a month getting up to the dozen; after which, my ranks increased with singular rapidity. Seeing many strange faces, I inquired of Roberto whence they came; and he told me that many of the new visiters were from villages five or six miles distant, it having been bruited that, at noon each day, all applicants were accommodated with a *grano* apiece by the *American admiral.* By this fact alone, you learn the extreme poverty of the poor and the value of money in this country.

We went on recruiting, until I now daily review some forty or fifty *gaberlunzies.* As my time here is limited, I have determined to persevere, and the only precaution taken is to drive off those who do not seem worthy to be enrolled on a list so eminently mendicant; for a good many of the wives of the fishermen began to appear in our ranks. A new-comer from Sta. Agata, a village across the mountains, had the indiscretion lately, as he got his *grano*, to wish me only a hundred years of life. "A hundred years!" repeated the king of the gang; "you blackguard, do you wish a signore who gives you a *grano* every day, only a hundred years? Knock him down! away with him!" "*Mille anni, signore,* – a thousand years; may you live a thousand years!" shouted the blunderer, amid some such tumult as one would see around a kettle of maccaroni in the streets of Naples, were its contents declared free. "A thousand years, and *long* ones too."*

On the People

MAKSIM GORKY, *Selected Letters* (1997)

From a letter of 23 June 1925

When I think about Russian literature, I want to return home. But I am still only learning to write. I've begun work on a huge novel [*The Life of Klim Samgin*]; it starts in the 1880s, I want it to close with 1918. I'm excited, all a-tremble, and now my hand has taken to aching, damn it. I've been working eight hours and more a day...

As for Italy, there's nothing to be said. Nature here is pretty, as everyone knows well enough. The people could be better, but they don't give much sign of striving particularly boldly towards that end...

On Environmental Horrors

HERBERT M. VAUGHAN, *The Naples Riviera* (1925)

... In the heavily perfumed air at dusk, or when the bright moonlight is flooding the whole scene and is turning the Bay into a mirror of molten silver, the song of the innumerable nightingales can be heard resounding from all sides; alas! too often sweet songs of sorrow for nests despoiled by the ruthless hands of young Sorrentine imps, as in the days of the Georgics.

> "Qualis populeâ maerens Philomela sub umbrâ
> Amissos queritur fetus, quos durus arator
> Observans nido implumes detraxit, at illa
> Flet noctem, ramoque sedens miserabile carmen
> Integrat, et moestis late loca questibus implet."

> ("At nightfall hear sad Philomel upraise
> Her mellow notes amid the dark-leaved bays,
> Mourning her babes and desecrated bower,

---

* The writer kept up his mendicant corps until he left Sorrento, there being no less than ninety-six paraded in the court the day he departed. Many of these poor people came ten miles! Some of them, he was told, passed the last week of his residence in Sorrento, in order to receive the pittance more at their ease. [Cooper's footnote.]

Which some rough peasant robbed in evil hour;
She tells her story of despair and love,
Until her plaintive music fills the grove.")

All is fragrant, warm, genial, and peaceful, save for the melancholy notes of poor ill-used Philomel, who is foolish enough to visit a cruel country, wherein every bird is merely regarded as a toothsome morsel for the family pot. We bird-lovers of Britain, with our Selborne Societies and our Wild Birds' Protection Acts, find it extremely difficult to understand the utter indifference displayed by Italians of all classes, towards the feathered race. The whole of the beautiful country with its cypress hedges and olive groves lies almost mute and lifeless, for on every festival the fields and lanes are patrolled by bands of *cacciatori* with dogs and guns on the look-out for game, if blackbirds and sparrows can be accounted such. In some districts it is even dangerous for pedestrians to use the roads on a Sunday, for fear of a stray bullet, since all, as a rule, fire recklessly at any creature within and out of range. Nor is this senseless war of extermination carried on merely with guns, for trapping is used extensively, and very ingenious and elaborate are some of the arts employed in this wretched quest. Every country house has its *uccellare*, or snare for the securing of small birds for the table, whilst many of the parish priests in the mountain districts add to their scanty incomes by catching the fledglings which the young peasants sell in the neighbouring market. The result is what might only naturally be expected – a scarcity of birds and an almost complete absence of song, for the whole countryside has been practically denuded of black-birds and thrushes; even the nightingale has escaped destruction rather on account of its nocturnal habits than of its tiny size and exquisite notes. It is positively sickening to observe the quantities of slaughtered wild birds in an Italian market at any season of the year, for the work of devastation proceeds apace equally in spring time. Basketfuls of thrushes and blackbirds, and strings of smaller varieties – linnets, sparrows, robins, finches, even the diminutive gold-finches, most beautiful, most gay, and most innocent of all songsters – are being hawked about by leathern-lunged *contadini*, who, alas! always manage to find customers in plenty. No matter how melodious, how lovely, or how useful to the farmer a bird may be, no Italian, high or low, seems to have any sense or appreciation of its merits except as an article of food; it is merely a thing that requires to be caught, killed, cooked and eaten, and Providence has decreed its existence for no other purpose; even gold-finches in the eye of an Italian look better served on a skewer than when they are flying round the thistle-heads, uttering their bright musical notes and enlivening the dead herbage of winter with their gay plumage. *Che bel arrosto!* (what a glorious dish!) sigh the romantic peasants, as they glance upward for a moment from their labour in the fields at the sound of the larks carolling overhead; and though an educated Italian would probably not give vent to so vulgar a remark, he would much prefer the *bel arrosto* to the "profuse strains of unpremeditated art" that so entrance the northerner, who is in reality far more of a poet by nature than the more picturesque dweller of the South. *Tantum pro avibus.*

NORMAN DOUGLAS, *Siren Land* (1911)

... The wooded tracts above Siren land... are an historical monument worth preserving: they display the flora of the Italian continent as it was in the days when the pious Aeneas sailed hitherwards. We are apt to forget that the whole appearance of Italian scenery has been changed owing to imported plants – the very cypress, the orange and maize and a hundred others great and small, which we regard as so characteristic, are aliens to the soil.* And the idea of preserving such tracts, absurd as it may seem to modern Italians, is really not inherently preposterous: certain civilized nations, such as the French, Americans, and English, have already by private gift or public subscription enclosed delectable woodlands to be an eternal delight and precept to their children; and only the other day the German Emperor rescued, in the very heart of Italy, the hoary oaks of Olevano from their impending fate. These, unless I am much mistaken, will be monuments more acceptable and more intelligible to posterity than the forests now growing up in Italy: forests of trousered political nonentities in bronze and marble, whose doctrines, often enough, became a derision before their protagonists were yet fairly in their graves.

The stealthy teachings of the sea, the Sirens' abode, still lie open to all, but those of earth-nature have been sadly misread of late and thwarted; and although we have heard much concerning the hygienic and economic advantages of properly controlled woodlands, there is room for another benefactor to mankind – for him, namely, who would proclaim their ethical significance, their influence as a refining and civilizing agency in the education of the human race. Who will deny that forests, once they have abandoned their hostile attitude to man's progress upon earth, exercise a benignant power, subtle and profound, upon the mind of a people; that music, architecture, and other generous arts have in forests sought, and found, high inspiration; that some of the sublimest efforts of literary genius could not have been conceived in regions as denuded of timber as Italy, Greece, and Spain now are?... I cannot but think that in sweeping away woodlands many deeply rooted humane aspirations, interwoven in their leafy solitudes, are likewise swept away, and a legion of gracious phantoms, who wandered freely among those solemn aisles ready to converse with all, banished for evermore. Shakespeare's England can still be found by those who look for it, but they who would discover the Italy of her poets must go far afield. Communion with nature, which exalts and purifies the mind, has ceased and in its place has arisen that pest of the South: futile inquisitiveness concerning man in his meanest manifestations.

*So, for instance, the spiky agave which they call mal'occhio because its point is a defence against the evil eye; the mesembryanthemum, known as unghia di lannara (witches' claws) from the shape of its leaves; or the grotesque Indian fig – one of God's earliest attempts at tree-making – which Preller, by mistake, depicted in his "Homeric landscape." The kaktos of the Greeks seems to have been a kind of artichoke. [Douglas' footnote.]

On Tourists

F. Marion Crawford, *Coasting by Sorrento and Amalfi* (1894)

... The song of songs is still unwritten, though nature's music makes man's grandest symphonies ridiculous, and sounds night and morning of the ears of him who has ears to hear.

But those are not the ears of the Cook's tourist, the German water-color painter, or the English spinster, all of whom come yearly southward to the Sorrento coast, as regular in their migration as the swallow, and far more welcome to the bankrupt hotel-keeper and the starving boatman, though less suggestive of poetic thoughts when a prominent object in the landscape. They come, they eat, they sleep, and their scarlet guide-books catch the sun and mark them for the native's prey. And then, thank heaven! they go. But it is easy to get away from them, for they keep to the beaten track, a vast flock of sheep for most of whose actions Mr. John Murray of Albemarle street will be held responsible at the last judgment. It may be doubted whether any church, any creed, or any despotic form of government which the world has ever seen, has disposed more completely of men's consciences, men's money, and men's movements, than the compilers and publishers of famous guide-books. Mr. Murray says to the tourist, "Go," and he goeth, or, "Do this," and he doeth it, in the certain consciousness that he cannot do wrong, which is more than the spiritual pastors and masters of the world generally succeed in accomplishing without assistance. I will not venture to impugn the judgment of the great guide-books, but I will venture to say that the average tourist in Italy sees very little that is distinctively Italian. The places he visits have been visited by such an infinite number of tourists before him that they have acquired a certain tourist color, so to say, and have suffered a certain localization of small iniquity which passes in the eyes of foreigners for native character. The least prejudiced of tourists is perhaps the German artist. He is also as a rule the most ready to undergo small hardships and considerable fatigue in the pursuit of the beautiful. But even he sees little. To him Capri seems wild, Naples picturesque, and Vesuvius romantic, and when he has painted the Capri Needles, has eatcn shell-fish at Santa Lucia, and has picked up a handful of scoriae on the edge of the crater, he has generally had his fill of southern Italy, and goes home to talk about it. So far as Sorrento is concerned, he and his colleagues in the land come to the most beautiful place in the world, stay three days in the modern hotel, drive a dozen miles or so over a modern road in a particularly shaky modern carriage, read "Agnes of Sorrento," and go to the next place mentioned in the guide-book...

On a Sense of Isolation

ALEXIS DE TOCQUEVILLE, *Memoir, Letters, and Remains* (1862)

From a letter of 5 January 1851

The worst part of my present residence is, that one may study everything but Italy. I should like to learn, at least, what is going on close to me in this little space; but I find it very difficult. Fear, ignorance or perfect indifference, closes every mouth. Besides, I find it hard to make acquaintances, though I am not particular as to the sort. The Italian middle classes, the only class to be found at Sorrento, do not care to visit you, because they do not care that you should visit them; and they do not care that you should visit them, because they live in garrets of which they are ashamed, and which they do not choose to convert into clean and comfortable apartments. You know, too, as well as I do, that conversation, especially in travelling, is an exchange, and that one can learn nothing from those who wish to learn nothing from you. How willingly I would allow these people to dispense with their low bows and their superlatives, if they would change them for the curiosity and precise information of those long Yankees, who used to go on chewing their tobacco while they were talking to us; but who every day taught us something that was new and useful.

I, therefore, learn only what my eyes teach me; and practical observation every day shows me that the population among whom I live is civil, well-behaved, easily led, not given to thieving, extremely ignorant and superstitious; in fact, in perpetual childhood. They are children of good dispositions, but ill brought up. Such a government as this could not be maintained with any other subjects. It is only on near view that one sees this. But how sad it is that, all the world over, governments are just as rascally as nations will allow them to be. This is the only limit to their vices...

On Political Unease and Repression

HENRIK IBSEN, *The Correspondence* (1970)

From a letter of 21 October 1867

We and the Bergsöe family have followed each other about all summer. Of course he and I often meet; but we are not the least likely ever to become close, intimate friends. We have both to blame for this. I shall not discuss the question of what the hindrance is on my side. In Bergsöe's nature there is much that is good; but I do not think it would do him any harm to be possessed of a little more character, conviction, and independence... He has had a tolerably disturbed summer – in Ischia the earthquake fright, cholera in Naples, brigands at Sorrento, and now war with Garibaldians here, and wrecked railways in the Papal States!

In spite of the disturbed state of the country, however, we go next week viâ Pompeii and Naples to Rome, to spend the winter there. It is not easy to predict what will be the result of the political events, but a settlement must certainly come soon.

ALEXIS DE TOCQUEVILLE, *Memoir, Letters, and Remains* (1862)

From a letter of 22 December 1850

... And as for this country, I have too near and too correct a view of it to like to speak of it. It is sad enough to live here, I assure you, for a man in search of anything but health; and even for those who, like me, are determined to seek nothing else, the enjoyment of good health is often spoiled by the sight of so much moral sickness. Like all my contemporaries, I have acquired, not only the taste for liberty, but the habit of it – a habit which, with many people, survives even the taste. I cannot reconcile myself to living, even as a foreigner, in a country in which every conceivable liberty is either restrained or destroyed. You, who have always lived in the midst of the animation, the independence, and the noise of our society, cannot understand the moral and intellectual torture experienced in a country where every action is hampered and impeded; where not only men are silent, but where even their thoughts are paralyzed. My mind seems to suffer, as my body did ten months ago, when my lungs played ill, and I could never take a full respiration.

Again, Italy is not China. It joins on to France; and though it does not greatly influence us, we act on it with enormous power. I cannot contemplate the miserable conditions into which it has fallen, without reflecting sadly on the fatal influence which we often exercise upon all around us. When a revolution breaks out in France, all Europe falls into anarchy; and when order is reëstablished in France, every other country restores the old abuses. We must confess that neighboring nations love us no better than their sovereigns do. The Revolution of 1848 has done irreparable injury to Italy. It precipitated her into a political movement which had no chance of success, unless the process were slow; and it tore the country out of the hands of the liberals to place it in those of the revolutionists. One is shocked to see how many germs of liberty have been miserably wasted, trodden under foot, and destroyed in this unhappy country, during the last three years, by those who had always liberty on their lips. I do not think that human folly and perversity ever showed themselves so openly.

I turn my eyes from such spectacles as much as I can, and try to create for myself a world of my own, consisting only of these lovely shores and of these fine skies...

Afterword
IMPRESSIONS OF SORRENTO TODAY, AND TOMORROW...

by

PORTIA PREBYS

The very first time one sees Sorrento is an unforgettable occasion: this magnificent sight leaves its indelible impression with us, forever. Even when we have moved on elsewhere, or returned home, that view is still there, in one's heart and soul, and is part, immediately, of one's deepest dreams. It cannot be duplicated anywhere else in the world.

Most travelers today arrive in Sorrento by private car or motor coach from Naples, working their way out of the populous and chaotic metropolis, through the jumble of broken-down constructions that crush in on the modern highway, southward, toward the Sorrentine Peninsula which juts out into the sea between the Bay of Naples and the Bay of Salerno.

Of a sudden, on either side of the winding road, luxuriant foliage becomes the dominant feature, ramblings of green up and over stark gray and white rock formations that surge upward into the blue cobalt sky or drop sharply outward toward the even bluer sapphire sea. Orange and lemon groves, with their shiny, waxy leaves, fill every corner of the landscape, their golden fruit hanging close to century-old gnarled branches. Olive orchards lie there in contrast, with their gray and silver opaque leaves catching every breeze. Grape vines grow every which way, up and down the rocky dividing walls, on either side of the road, forming bowers laden with heavy bunches of ripening grapes.

Tradition has it that once you have seen the Bay of Naples, you have seen the most beautiful scenery in the world outside of paradise. Its beauty is based on the bright sun sparkling over the deep blue water, reflecting the grays, whites, and neutrals of the stark rock formations on the Sorrentine Peninsula, echoing the shadows set by Vesuvius, catching the light of the shimmering buildings off in the distance of downtown Naples. This is no common sea, and Sorrento is no common sea resort, a part of Italy, and yet no common part.

In all of Italy, the family endures as the most important cultural unit within society. According to John Grimond, foreign editor of *The Economist,* the primacy of the family

> explains the lack of public spirit in Italy, and even of the concept of the public good. It partly explains the existence of *correnti* in political parties, in which alliances are based not on principle but on the loyalty and trust owed to an individual. It explains the kinship or *parentela* system of dealing with the bureaucracy: find a crony, or, better still, a relation, and get him to fix things for you. It explains the Mafia, the biggest family of them all... It also explains the pattern of business. From the Agnelli's down, Italians like to keep control of their affairs within the family. They are therefore reluctant to put their companies on the stockmarket and risk losing control.

> [*The Economist*, 26 May 1990, p. 14]

Modern Sorrentine life is based on the family, too, but the notion is enlarged to include all of Sorrento and environs as family. The concept of public good, a public good for the good of Sorrento, is extended from family to family in order to guarantee the best possible conditions for Sorrento's largest industry: tourism. Every single citizen is openly proud of the town, and who would not be proud of such a special place?

The people of Sorrento have been receiving visitors in their home town for over two thousand years. They welcome the traveler and provide hospitality like few other natives in resorts that I have visited around the world, and, yet, they are still hosts, planners of the experience for the visitor-guests. Shopkeepers, waiters, ice cream sellers, gardeners – no one ever shows impatience with the traveler; no one gets surly or complains about a tiny tip, a modest purchase, or interminable questions about how to get somewhere. There is no hard sell in any of the shops, no anxious comments or angry invectives, no hurried disattention, no restless remarks. The shops and restaurants that I observed are Sorrentine-owned, unlike in other Italian tourist areas, and locally staffed.

The "extended family" has identified tourism as its common good for almost two hundred years, appearing in sundry forms, true, but consistently present. The Sorrentines keep their identity and dignity, and have done so throughout it all, but recognize that future tourism depends on them, on the treatment handed out to every guest, in every way, on the impression that each traveler takes home after a visit to Sorrento. Hospitality facilitators, they offer their unique town and the unique experience of being there.

After all, Sorrento is not just any seaside resort. It is the best one in southern Italy, and, perhaps, any place in the world. The paradise, then, is theirs to propose, partially their creation, and they present it with an expertise that has been polished and refined over time.

Mary McCarthy pointed out a half-century ago (in *Venice Observed*) that Venice, one of Italy's noted tourist attractions, is a "folding picture-postcard of itself," not like the Venetians themselves, famously proud and aloof, who show ill-concealed contempt for the tourists on whom they so totally depend. The tourist Venice *is* Venice and it is truly foolish to think otherwise. And yet, how many travelers leave Venice with a bad taste in their mouth? Yes, an interesting experience, a weekend in Venice, but quite a hassle, too, in every way: restaurants that charge according to timed presence, glass hawkers and aggressive gondola drivers, interminable lines everywhere. I have the impression that these hassles do not often take place in Sorrento, where a culture kind to the consumer (and we must call the modern traveler a "consumer") prevails. The picture postcard exists, but visitors hope to mail a few from Sorrento more than once in their lifetimes.

In downtown Florence, it is disconcerting to dine in jewels of modern restaurants, decorated with the latest, most fashionable amenities and furniture, only to find that the owner is an American, a Pole, a Slav, or an Argentine, the chef is Egyptian, and the waiters are French or German or Irish. Not so in Sorrento: it would not be productive for the community, because outsiders are not part of the long tradition of treating the traveler with kid gloves and their loyalties could lie elsewhere. Yes, a living can be made, a good living at that, but to aim for a financial killing would ruin the town's long-term viability for posterity.

The proprietor of a restaurant in downtown Sorrento told me recently that his establishment has been in family hands for over one hundred years, that their business is really keeping the visitor happy by providing first-quality fare in a unique setting. The terraced orange grove that is the lusciously green garden in which dining takes place all year around in his establishment is peculiarly Sorrentine, a true paradise for the diner in every sense of the word. Friendly local waiters who carry on in local lingo, soft gliding Italian and perfect English, pride themselves on their relationship with the owner and his family and the fact that they are extremely fortunate to be able to spend their entire working career in a single establishment. Hearing them speak about their own personal status simply underlines the fact that they are living the best life possible in their estimation. Here I must disagree with Marion Crawford when he claims that "the average tourist sees very little that is distinctly Italian." This restaurant *is* Italian, from the Antico Ginori dinnerware in four colors hanging in the entrance, to the antique majolica decorating the garden wall down to every last item on the menu. And so too, each in its unique way, are other Sorrentine restaurants.

When questioned about why they enjoy living in Sorrento, the local citizen invariably responds that Sorrento is *tranquilla*. Tranquil as an answer does not necessarily mean quiet or peaceful, but, rather, for them, free from the hassle of thievery, pickpockets, vandals, young hoodlums feeling their oats, vagrants. Sorrento is free, that is, of what have come to be Italian traditions elsewhere, the tradition of drive-by purse snatchings by thugs on powerful, recklessly-driven motorcycles, for example. The visitor notices the absence of vandalism to property, of car antitheft alarms, of signatures spray-painted on houses, of graffiti in the public bathrooms or on the platforms of the Circumvesuviana Station. Three-year olds leave home alone to go down the street to the neighborhood kindergarten, older children play everywhere in town, unattended, and, yet, protected by the guardian glances of the townspeople. Sorrentine women walk the streets wearing gold necklaces and bracelets without fear. The individual person and property are respected.

This enviable state of affairs is part of what locals feel is necessary to protect the tourist, and the tourist industry: the Sorrentines dictate and will not lose control. Their streets are clean, their homes and hotels immaculate and comfortable. There are many public gardens with benches on which to rest and enjoy the daily scene. The people are genuinely *nice,* and a sense of great hospitality prevails. Arch rivals of Naples, the Sorrentines aim to score in tourism where Naples fails due to its size, the seemingly permanent chaos, corruption, and general lack of concern for others. Again, this paradise belongs to the Sorrentines and they offer it to us in style.

Tolerance for others is an obvious principle on which modern Sorrento is built. Many families have welcomed foreigners as sons- and daughters-in-law, adopted children from abroad. Plurality promotes international understanding and the Sorrentines are all for it, not instinctively suspicious of the outsider. The visitor does not witness the dangerous collision between generations and traditions that exists in other parts of Italy. If it exists, it is played out behind closed doors. A strong cultural tension seems to move the young people along, a plurality of values that can only be achieved by openness to others, to outside ideas and challenges. Not all of the old-fashioned certainties have disappeared here.

Traditionally, Italy has been a country of emigration and, yet, almost no one you meet here feels it is necessary to go abroad to earn a living. The family, extended as it may be, has met the challenge and managed to keep most everyone home to welcome the world traveler as visitor and connoisseur in their Garden of Eden.

Sources Cited

J. Howe Adams. "The Highroad from Salerno to Sorrento." In *The Century – Illustrated Monthly Magazine.* 48, 337-340. 1894.

Isaac Babel. Letters. In Nathalie Babel. *Isaac Babel: The Lonely Years 1925-1939.* New York: Farrar, Straus & Company. 1964.

Robert Browning. "The Englishman in Italy." In *Dramatic Romances.* London, no publisher. 1845.

James Fenimore Cooper. *Excursions in Italy,* Vol. I. London: Richard Bentley. New Burlington Street. 1838.

F. Marion Crawford. "Coasting by Sorrento and Amalfi." In *The Century – Illustrated Monthly Magazine.* 48, 324-336. 1894.

–. *To Leeward.* New York: P. F. Collier. 1892.

Norman Douglas. "Mr Marion Crawford." In *Looking Back: An Autobiographical Excursion.* New York: Harcourt, Brace and Company. 1933.

–. *Siren Land.* London: Secker & Warburg. 1911.

Sybil Fitzgerald. *Naples: Painted by Augustine Fitzgerald, Described by Sybil Fitzerald.* London: Adam & Charles Black. 1904.

André Gide. *The Journals of André Gide*, Vol. III (1928-1939). Translated by Justin O'Brien. New York: Alfred A. Knopf. 1949.

J. W. Goethe. *Goethe's Works*, Vol. III. Philadelphia: G. Barrie. 1885.

Maksim Gorky. *Maksim Gorky: Selected Letters.* Translated and edited by Andrew Barratt and Barry P. Scherr. Oxford: Clarendon Press. 1997.

Augustus J. C. Hare. *Cities of Southern Italy and Sicily.* London: George Allen. 1891.

Henrik Ibsen. *The Correspondence of Henrik Ibsen.* Edited by Mary Morison, 1905. New York: Haskell House Publishers Ltd. 1970.

Julia Kavanagh. *A Summer and Winter in the Two Sicilies*, Vol. I. London: Hurst and Blackett. 1858.

Walter Savage Landor. *The Complete Works*, Vol. III, *Imaginary Conversations.* London: Blackwoods. 1843.

Friedrich Nietzsche. *Briefe 1875-1879.* Edited by Giorgio Colli and Mazzino Montinari. Berlin and New York: Walter de Gruyter. 1980.

Arthur H. Norway. *Naples, Past and Present*, Vol. II. New York: Frederick A. Stokes Co. 1901.

John Ruskin. *The Diaries of John Ruskin,* Vol. I (1835-1847). Edited by Joan Evans and John Howard Whitehouse. Oxford: At the Clarendon Press. 1956.

Mary Wollstonecraft Shelley. *The Letters of Mary Wollstonecraft Shelley,* Vol. III. Edited by Betty T. Bennett. Baltimore: Johns Hopkins University Press. 1988.

W. J. A. Stamer. *Dolce Napoli.* London: Charing Cross Publishing Company, Ltd. 1878.

Statius. "The Villa of Pollius Felix at Surrentum." In *Sylvae,* II. 2. Translated by J. H. Mozley. London: William Heinemann Ltd. 1928.

Harriet Beecher Stowe. *Agnes of Sorrento.* Boston and New York: Houghton, Mifflin and Company. 1890.

Henry Swinburne. *Travels in the Two Sicilies in the Years 1777, 1778, 1779, and 1780,* Vol. I. London: J. David-P. Elmsly. 1790.

Alexis de Tocqueville. *Memoir, Letters, and Remains of Alexis de Tocqueville,* Vol. II. Boston: Ticknor and Fields. 1862.

Herbert M. Vaughan. *The Naples Riviera.* London: Methuen & Co. 1925.

Cosima Wagner. *Cosima Wagner's Diaries,* Vol. I (1869-1877). Edited by Martin Gregor-Dellin and Dietrich Mack. Translated by Geoffrey Skelton. New York and London: Harcourt Brace Jovanovich. 1978.

Richard Wagner. *Letters of Richard Wagner*, Vol. II. Edited by Wilhelm Altmann. Translated by M. M. Bozman. London & Toronto: J. M. Dent & Sons, Ltd. 1927.

Index of Authors

Index of Illustrations

Finito di stampare
nel mese di luglio 2000
da "La Buona Stampa" Napoli
per conto della Franco Di Mauro Editore